Charade

THE COVID LIES THAT CRUSHED A NATION

David Marcus

A BOMBARDIER BOOKS BOOK
An Imprint of Post Hill Press
ISBN: 978-1-63758-303-6
ISBN (eBook): 978-1-63758-187-2

Charade:
The Covid Lies That Crushed A Nation
© 2021 by David Marcus
All Rights Reserved

Cover Design by Tiffani Shea

This book contains research and commentary about COVID-19, which is classified as an infectious disease by the World Health Organization. Although every effort has been made to ensure that any medical or scientific information present within this book is accurate, the research about COVID-19 is still ongoing.

Post Hill Press
New York • Nashville
posthillpress.com

Published in the United States of America
1 2 3 4 5 6 7 8 9 10

TO LIBBY

Table Of Contents

Prologue

---◇---

The Charade

A charade is very different from a magic trick. The latter is a mere illusion. Where did the rabbit come from? How did you know what card I chose? The former, the charade, is multifarious, all consuming—it envelops one until they do not know the truth from fiction, until all of reality is entwined with the canard. For most of the year of our Lord 2020, which often felt more like His wrath than His love, Americans were living in a charade, a "new normal" as some called it. As we begin to fully understand the devastating effects of our response to the Coronavirus, the toll of our lockdowns, we must first unravel what happened to us and understand how we came to accept it.

There was one great central lie of the Coronavirus crisis, a pernicious yet seemingly encouraging phrase: "We are all in this together." This was simply never true. Those who could work from home were not "in it" with those who found themselves without a paycheck; those for whom the $1,200 stimulus check was like a spring bonus were not in it with those who had to make it linger for months. The scientists and experts who warned, often times correctly, about the extreme approaches taken by our government and were mocked and called evil were not in it with the beloved and glorified public health officials heralded by the media. So varied were our experiences, in fact, state by state, city by city, that we wound up in some sense with two Americas, one resembling the functioning society of the old normal, and another the restrictive new normal of a shut-down country. And we arrived at two American populations, one ready to stay home at a moment's instruction from the state and one more jealous of their basic rights as understood in the "old normal."

The word charade is a relative newcomer to the English language, entering the lexicon in the late 18th century. One modern definition is as follows. "An absurd pretense intended to create a pleasant or respectable appearance." So, for example, keeping millions of kids out of school for months at a time was not talked about as child abuse, but rather the soothing "stay home, stay safe." The permanent shuttering of a third of small businesses was not called an economic disaster, but rather "stopping the spread." Surges in suicides, drug addiction, depression, and domestic abuse were not spoken of as horrifying crises, but rather "doing our part."

Early on in the crisis, to even mention the downsides of lockdown as anything more than a trifling inconvenience was met with accusations of trying to kill Grandma. Even by the time that some, mostly on the Right, came to fight back against pandemic correctness and speak the names of those downsides, the whole thing had become so mired in the politics of the presidential election that no rational balance could emerge. As with so much of our society and culture under his presidency, Donald Trump was the central figure and focus of a pandemic that was obviously much larger than him or his leadership. In all honesty, one of the great tragedies of the crisis was that it occurred in an election year: both sides had perverse interests to overstate or understate the threat of the virus.

But ultimately, this was not primarily a story about Washington, DC or the federal government. Every state, even every city or small town, took a different approach. Governors became heroes or villains depending on the bias of the media outlet discussing them. Results, both medical and economic, in each state were cherry-picked to pretend that one approach or another were the obvious and true correct ones. In fact, to the extent that the results varied, and they didn't actually vary that much, judging them is a subjective endeavor.

There is, of course, a game we all know called charades, one in which we act out an object or idea without saying it. And performance too was central to the pandemic response. Masks, for example, became more than just an effort at mitigating the spread of the disease; they were worn also as a signal that one took the virus seriously. They were even worn in social media profile pictures, as if breath could flow from a laptop or cell phone screen. Among many, a performative nonchalance flowered, "It's not so bad," they would say, but they did not tend to be people waiting hours in breadlines that looked like colorized copies of some 1930s photograph.

By the end of 2020, more than three hundred thousand Americans would succumb to the Coronavirus, the vast majority elderly or infirm, but this was much more than a medical crisis. In most places, scarcely any aspects of our lives were left untouched by it. This is not a story about a disease: it is not a story about government; it is not a story about the media, or individual lives; it is a story about everything. And it has not ended. There is a profound purpose to looking back over what happened to us all in 2020, painful though some things may be to remember. In judging the mistakes, as well as the heroism, in examining the successes and the far too frequent failures of our response to the virus from China, we can learn not merely how to better handle the next pandemic that may come, but also what freedom means to us going forward.

In a nation founded on fundamental individual rights, how many of those rights can be rescinded because of a public health crisis? And what exactly constitutes a public health crisis? Under what circumstances can the state deny you the right to leave your home, to operate a business, to go to church, and to send your kids to school? In the 225-year history of the United States of America, never has everyone, every single citizen, been simultaneously compelled to obey the edicts and diktats of government in the way we just experienced. So let us look back with cool and rational eyes at this charade and decide if we should ever allow the like to happen again.

Chapter 1

The Last Days of Normalcy

CPAC is one of those things that everyone loves to drag on but is actually a lot of fun. Founded in 1974, just like me, the Conservative Political Action Conference is a hive of the Right's brightest luminaries and loser lowlifes. The best and the worst are on display like some kind of bizarre social science fair. I've only been twice. Once in 2017, just weeks after President Trump was inaugurated, and the last time in late February, 2020, just weeks before the beginning of the recent unpleasantness.

Shortly upon arriving at the Gaylord National Resort and Convention Center in Maryland, I saw Mollie Hemingway in one of the lobby areas. Mollie is a senior editor on my home team the *Federalist* and as usual, she had a crowd around her offering well wishes. When I went up to her, she offered me her forearm for something along the lines of a forearm bump, something not dissimilar from what Jose Canseco and Mark McGwire used to do.

That was the first time my behavior was ever modified by the Novel Coronavirus from China. We had talked about the virus with varying degrees of alarm for the previous few weeks in our news meetings and the public knew something about it, but at the time of CPAC, it was mostly joked about. As of me sitting here writing this on a scorching hot July Brooklyn day, CPAC was the last time I was in a room with more than one hundred people.

Inez Stepman of the International Women's Forum had asked me to be on a panel about how conservatives can compete in the culture space along with Saagar Enjeti and Spencer Brown. Inez and her husband, the author Jarret Stepman, had been kind enough to put me up at their lovely DC apartment. A charming evening of cocktails, conversation, and Soviet 1980s punk music ensued. There was even a roof deck where I could smoke. In the morning, it was off to the Gaylord.

The first event of the day was a hoot. It was a brunch-type deal hosted by Facebook. The vibe was very "What? We love you conservatives. It's all good—have a mimosa." We were assured that our concerns regarding the targeting of conservatives for shadow bans and such were of the highest priority to them and we all got ceramic Facebook to-go coffee mugs. Libby Emmons, my wife from whom I am separated, was there with her team from *The Post Millennial*, where she is a senior editor. We all had quite a merry time.

I very much enjoy being on panels. Prior to stumbling almost accidently into journalism about seven years ago, I had spent almost twenty years in the New York City theater world. Libby and I ran a theater company we cofounded together during this time called Blue Box Productions. Yes, hence my twitter handle. I acted in dozens of plays for our company as well as many others around Gotham. What I miss most about it is feeling the energy of a crowd, a house, and panels give me something like that.

As an actor, it is difficult to overstate the difference between a large and a small house when you are performing. When I was first studying at NYU in the early 1990s, I chose the Practical Aesthetics studio founded by David Mamet, which is now known as the Atlantic Theater Company Studio. Mamet was a hero of mine but within about two weeks, I started souring on what he was selling. I believed at that time that acting was a matter of blocking out the audience and existing in the moment on stage as if it were really, truly happening. Mamet had other ideas.

For Mamet, acting was a kind of grift, and you can't be a grifter without dealing with your mark. Under the rubric of his technique, the audience was always to be there in your mind. I didn't care for it and left for the friendly confines of the more traditionally method acting based Stella Adler Studio. And yes, on more than one occasion, I pretended to be an ice cream cone.

It would take me a decade to learn that, surprise surprise, Mamet was right. Only as I worked more with larger and larger audiences did I come to understand what he had been teaching. There is a physical energy that the house brings: you almost hear their heartbeats; there is aspect to being observed that triggers response. A theater actor is in a symbiotic relationship with the audience.

One of the best plays I ever did was Len Jenkin's *Margo Veil: An Entertainment*, at the Flea Theater. It's a brilliantly written, or wrought, show that was directed by the playwright. The *New York Times* compared our cast of eight to the original cast of *Saturday Night Live*, which, you know, that's pretty good.

I had a long, elaborate monologue in which I played an illicit businessman of some kind who was trapped in Lithuania and had lost his pants. The speech was directed over the phone to his secretary back in the states, with whom he was also obviously flirting. Toward the end of the call, he tries to reassure her that he will be back soon. "I'll be back Thursday—we'll go out, dinner, a movie." Each performance,

I would pick a woman in the audience and deliver that line directly to her. One night, the woman looked me in the eyes and mouthed, "OK." That's Mamet-style acting.

All of this is to say that months removed from the last time I was in a crowd of people, it has become clear just how much we lose when we deny ourselves human contact. That last sea of faces I saw from the panel stage were unmasked, their visages registering what they were hearing and sending information back about how it impacted them. One cannot help but take for granted that which one has never been denied; this was a lesson everyone was soon to learn.

After the panel, I was invited to a *Townhall* drinks thing by my good friend Ellie Bufkin, who wrote there at the time. The room quickly filled up, speckled with conservative journos stirring their cocktails while Diamond and Silk signed autographs off in the corner. Most talk was of the election. This was also the Saturday of the South Carolina primary, which Joe Biden won in a landslide and which set the stage for him to basically secure the nomination a few days later on Super Tuesday.

Conventional wisdom as we sipped our drinks and nibbled on our tapas was that the primary would drag on mainly between Biden and Bernie Sanders for at least another month or two. We didn't know that within a day, Beto

O'Rourke and Amy Klobuchar would drop out and endorse Uncle Joe. It is hard to imagine what would have happened to the primary had South Carolina been closer and the contest was still up in the air in March. Most likely absolute chaos. A week earlier, Biden had truly seemed dead in the water. The Democrats dodged a dangerous bullet by securing their nominee before everything changed, before voting in person became potentially deadly, or so people would believe.

The evening wrapped up at an after-party in somebody's hotel room at the Gaylord. I got thrown out for some reason; maybe I was smoking on the balcony, which is weirdly still inside the glass walls that surround the giant campus. In any event, I dimly recall being ready to leave anyway. It had been a long day and I knew there would be no shortage of breaking news to cover the next morning, and probably brunch.

When Monday arrived, we had our start-of-the-week *Federalist* telephone meeting. This was the first time that the Chinese virus, as it was widely known then, had dominated the affair. We had talked about it since January when we discussed whether travel from China should be banned, something Trump would do on January 31. But over the ensuing weeks, it was more something to keep an eye on than something to actually cover intensely.

Now that changed. I recall Mollie and our new senior editor, Chris Bedford, being the ones forcefully saying that this thing could get really bad. I recall being dubious; it still didn't feel like it could be such an earth-shattering event. The stock market had taken a hit after the announcement of the travel ban, but entering March, it had recovered those losses. There was nothing in the psychological atmosphere of the country that felt like anything huge was about to happen. We knew that the Chinese Communist Party (CCP) had locked down Wuhan and had watched with amusement videos of drones warning people in the city to put on their masks. But as late as February 29, Dr. Anthony Fauci, then relatively unknown, would tell the *Today Show* that there was no need for Americans to change their behavior.

After the meeting, I was sufficiently shaken up to give Libby a call to discuss what we would do in what still seemed like the unlikely event that our son Charlie's school would shut down. In a conversation that parents across the country would be having much sooner rather than later, we worked out a plan to split the school days between our respective apartments, which are just blocks from each other. I still hoped that this would be a needless contingency; Libby, like Mollie and Bedford, seemed convinced the worst would soon be upon us. What can I say? I'm an optimist. I am, after all, the columnist who once wrote a piece about why then White

House Communications Director Anthony Scaramucci was the man that America and Donald Trump needed. About three hours after it ran, the Mooch had been fired. That kind of thing happens to me a lot.

On its March 1 cover, the *New York Times* ran what, in retrospect, was a rather cheery article titled, "How Prepared Is the U.S. for a Coronavirus Outbreak?" The answer seemed to be "pretty damn well prepared." According to the article,

"Much about the coronavirus remains unclear, and it is far from certain that the outbreak will reach severe proportions in the United States or affect many regions at once. With its top-notch scientists, modern hospitals and sprawling public health infrastructure, most experts agree, the United States is among the countries best prepared to prevent or manage such an epidemic."[1]

This is very important to keep in mind. Just a few months later, most of the media would insist that January and February had been wasted months during which the Trump administration should have been taking much more drastic action. What's curious about that is twofold. First of all, nobody seemed to know exactly what the administration should have been doing that it did not, and secondly, the Department of Health and Human Services had been working feverishly during that time to prepare for the worst.

In any event, by the time I got back to Brooklyn early that week, things seemed up in the air, but still calm. Troubling reports began seeping out of Italy, where cases and deaths were climbing steeply, but the biggest concerns there were about the availability of hospital beds and medical equipment. And we were learning that deaths from the virus were vastly more common among the elderly than the young. Here in the United States, we had only a handful of cases, mostly limited to nursing homes in Seattle.

It was just a few days later when the email from CPAC arrived.

"The American Conservative Union has learned that one of our CPAC attendees has unfortunately tested positive today for coronavirus. The exposure occurred previous to the conference. A New Jersey hospital tested the person, and CDC confirmed the positive result. The individual is under the care of medical professionals in the state of New Jersey, and has been quarantined."

It was hard to know what to make of it. A flurry of phone calls commenced between people I had seen there. As it turned out, I wasn't feeling very well upon getting back, but that isn't all that strange. For years, people had talked about the CPAC flu as a very real thing; after all, it's a close quarters convention in late February with lots of colds and bugs flitting about. My alcohol consumption over that few days had also been, well, shall we say not particularly moderate. I had been scheduled to go back to DC that Thursday to shoot what would be the last in-studio episode of *The McGlaughlin Group* prior to the lockdown. My symptoms combined with my potential exposure to this Chinese virus was enough to convince me that sitting in a room with Eleanor Clift, Pat Buchanan, and Clarence Page, each in the vulnerable age group, was not a good idea. My editor Emily Jashinsky, a regular on the show, subbed for me. I didn't realize that it would be five months until I would leave New York City again.

The New York City I returned to at the end of February was about to change, in many ways forever. By December, the immigrant-owned dry cleaner and tailor on my corner would be gone forever; who needed dry cleaning in a lockdown? A sign on the building read, "Coming Soon: Popeyes." You see, as in all things, there would be winners and losers. The country itself would undergo a crisis and trauma that was hard to even imagine at that time. By the fall, it would be common to hear people speak of the pre-Covid time, or the before time. Some kind of all-encompassing cultural debate would develop over the coming months about when, and eventually if, we would ever return to "normal." Or would we arrive at a "new normal?" Would people ever shake hands again?

Eventually, would people wear masks forever? But also political questions about what kind of emergency authority government can use, including denying constitutional rights for extended periods of time because of the pandemic, the crisis.

That crisis, the virus itself, as well as the lockdowns with their attendant economic and human costs occurred as a chaosmos of choices. Choices by President Trump, choices by governors, choices by advertisers and tech corporations, and ultimately, of course, choices by the American people themselves. The term chaosmos comes from Umberto Eco. It describes the work of James Joyce, particularly *Finnegans Wake*. It is a concept tied to the Middle Ages, the time of plague, and it sees the world as an ever-connected assembly of points, each tied to the other in real but unseen ways. Everything and everyone was about to change.

Chapter 2

Myth 1—The Wasted Months

There are two institutions primarily responsible for the unprecedented and bizarre screeching halt to life as we knew it that we all experienced in March of 2020. The first, of course, is the government—federal, state, and local—that unleashed the lockdown laws and set the standards for our quiet isolation. But it is important to remember that this lockdown was not so much enforced as it was consented to. There were rare occasions in which police had to break up gatherings, but for the most part, people obeyed the orders, and that was primarily the result of the second institution, the media.

There is no button in the Oval Office, or anywhere else, that shuts down nearly the entire United States economy in a space of two weeks. That it happened at all is like some kind of horrible miracle: on the one hand an amazing feat, on the other an invitation to abject economic devastation with accompanying human despair and loss. What such an action or event requires above all else is a myopia that colors every aspect of life in the hue of the crisis. In order to happen, the lockdown had to be the only thing happening.

All of this is what makes the story of the Coronavirus shutdown so difficult to tell and comprehend. As Shakespeare put it, "The eye sees not itself but by reflection." This storm was so vast, so all-encompassing, that we cannot get distance from it, we cannot see its wisping borders from the outside, and so to understand it, we must focus on the eye of the storm, the center from which it sprang into being. The first drops of the gathering storm began in far-flung Wuhan, China, in late 2019. It really wasn't until the last two weeks of December that the American news media began reporting on a mysterious Coronavirus in China's ninth-largest city. That nation had long been known as a hotspot for various forms of flu and virus thought to emerge from wet markets in which animals such as bats and pangolins are sold live in crowded areas. Indeed, when Dr. Deborah Birx, an HIV expert who was in Africa when she first caught wind of the virus, looked at the data, she assumed something along the lines of SARS was afoot. SARS is a serious disease, but not one that led to the shutdown of the global economy.

Before trying to assess what our government and media got wrong and what they got right, before handing out blame or lauding praise on this or that figure or outlet, before everything, it must be understood that the lies of the CCP put the entire world behind the eight ball. To make matters worse, the World Health Organization was eating up these lies like a Hungry Hungry Hippo and regurgitating them to the planet without the slightest reservation.

The reality of the deeply troubling relationship between China and the WHO would come to the fore in March, when a video showed a reporter from Hong Kong's RTHK news agency asking Bruce Aylward, a senior advisor to the WHO, about the possibility of Taiwan joining the organization, a move the CCP roundly opposes. Aylward first pretended not to hear the question. Then when it was asked again, he abruptly ended the video interview. It was a bizarre interaction that soon went viral. If an organization cannot even say the word "Taiwan" for fear of the Chinese government, what reasonable chance is there that they would express any reservations about data coming from China?

Though long suspected, the hard evidence of CCP duplicity would emerge in early May, when the Australian newspaper the *Daily Telegraph* obtained and reported on a fifteen-page Five Eyes report on the origins of the virus. Five Eyes is an intelligence alliance between the United States, Canada, Australia, the United Kingdom, and New Zealand. A kind of an anglophone spy club. Importantly, this wasn't just one intelligence agency with a potential political agenda; it was five of them, spread across countries with similar, though also varied interests. According to the *Daily Telegraph*, the report states that to the "endangerment of other countries," the Chinese government covered up news of the virus by silencing or disappearing doctors who spoke out, destroying evidence of it in laboratories and refusing to provide live samples to international scientists who were working on a vaccine.

By December, CNN would obtain and confirm a trove of leaked documents that showed without doubt that China had been lying from the beginning about the number of cases and the severity of the disease. These are all facts that China denies, but that many in the government and media had known and spoken about for months, as early as February, in fact. As evidence of the CCP's duplicity continues to emerge, the "wasted months" narrative is exposed as a myth.

All of this lying from China came in the midst of an extremely tense relationship between Washington and Beijing. It is important to remember that before the evening of November 8, 2016, which I like to call the "Massacre of Brooklyn," China had every reason to believe it was on the verge of sustaining a very lucrative status quo. Though both Hillary Clinton and Donald Trump opposed the Chinese-backed Trans-Pacific Partnership trade deal, Clinton had first called it the "gold standard," of trade deals before vowing to block it amid political pressure. The Chinese knew very well they would do better under Clinton than under a Trump who thought trade wars were "very easy to win." And they were right.

Even more tension was being generated by 2019 as a result of Chinese repressive actions toward protestors in Hong Kong and the alleged concentration camps filled with potentially a million or more Muslim ethnic minority Uyghurs. These controversies would soon sweep up American companies with strong ties and huge money interests with China. The NBA and Hollywood are still sputtering to find the right tone on Chinese human rights. The big hit app of the year, TikTok, which our teenagers took to in droves, would be accused of gathering information on Americans for the CCP; Trump would go so far as to threaten an American ban on the platform.

The degree to which politicians and the media were willing to place blame on the Chinese government became an early and important political fracture that would soon turn into a clean break regarding how to respond to the virus. The lines were clear; Democrats, their media allies, and Big Tech all were more sympathetic to China than American conservatives. Holding China responsible for its deceptions was something many on the left found difficult to do, even in the face of the mounting evidence. They had another villain in mind, one closer to home.

This change in China policy is an important backdrop to the story of the Coronavirus crisis. During the Post-Cold War period, the neoliberal assumption from both parties was that by opening up free trade with China, it would almost by osmosis become a more liberal and democratic nation. This was a project outlined in Francis Fukuyama's famous 1992 essay "The End of History?" The supposition was that the Cold War victory of free market democratic systems pointed the direction and laid out the roadmap that every country would eventually follow.

The upshot of these policies in the United States was an economic boom, but not for everyone; for American factory workers and others in manufacturing, all of this free trade was sending their jobs away. What Trump offered in 2016 was something very similar to Ross Perot's Reform Party in the 1990s, probably the most significant force pushing against neoliberalism up to that time. Perot failed, but his constituency of voters never vanished; they were still there, especially in places like the Rust Belt, and by the time Trump ran, they were the ones who secured his win. For China, this was very bad news indeed.

So with all of the strains between the two nations, it might not be surprising that China was less than forthcoming with information about the virus; that is not an excuse, obviously, but rather a geopolitical reality. Might China have been more willing for example to have American inspectors in Wuhan had the relations been warmer? Possibly. In the end, by the time the virus reached the United States, we had woefully inadequate information about it and very little time to figure things out. All of this makes it even more impressive that the Trump administration began standing up a response as quickly as it did.

In April, I obtained from Health and Human Services (HHS) a timeline of the administration response to the virus in January—just January—and as you will see, it looks like a CVS receipt.

December 31: CDC, including Director Robert Redfield, learns of a "cluster of 27 cases of pneumonia of unknown etiology" reported in Wuhan, China.

January 1: CDC begins developing situation reports, which are shared with HHS.

January 3: Director Redfield emails and speaks on the phone with Dr. George Gao, Director of the China Center for Disease Control and Prevention.

January 3: Director Redfield speaks with Secretary Alex Azar, and HHS notifies the National Security Council (NSC).

January 4: Director Redfield emails Dr. Gao again and offers CDC assistance, stating, "I would like to offer CDC technical experts in laboratory and epidemiology of respiratory infectious diseases to assist you and China CDC in identification of this unknown and possibly novel pathogen."

January 6: At the request of Secretary Azar, Director Redfield sends formal letter to China CDC offering full CDC assistance.

January 6: CDC issues a Level 1 Travel Watch for China.

January 6: National Institute of Allergy and Infectious Diseases (NIAID) Director Anthony Fauci begins doing interviews on the outbreak.[2]

January 7: CDC establishes a 2019-nCoV Incident Management Structure to prepare for potential U.S. cases and to support the investigation in China or other countries, if requested.

January 8: CDC distributes an advisory via the Health Alert Network, which communicates to state and local public health partners, alerting health care workers and public health partners of the outbreak.

January 9: CDC and FDA begin collaborating on a diagnostic test for the Novel Coronavirus.

January 10: China shares viral sequence, allowing NIH scientists to begin work on a vaccine that evening.

January 11: First Death Reported in China[3]

January 13: 41 Cases in China, First Case Reported Outside China[4]

January 13: NIH shares their vaccine sequence with a pharmaceutical manufacturer.

January 14: The National Security Council begins daily Novel Coronavirus Policy Coordination Council meetings.

January 14: WHO tweets: "Preliminary investigations conducted by the Chinese authorities have found no clear evidence of human-to-human transmission of the novel #coronavirus (2019-nCoV) identified in #Wuhan, #China."[5]

January 17: CDC and Customs and Border Protection began enhanced screening of travelers from Wuhan at three airports that receive significant numbers of travelers from that city, expanded in the following week to five airports, covering 75–80 percent of Wuhan travel.

January 17: CDC hosts its first telebriefing on the virus, with Dr. Nancy Messonnier, Director of the National Center for Immunization and Respiratory Diseases, who emphasizes "this is a serious situation" and "we know [from the experience of SARS and MERS that] it's crucial to be proactive and prepared."[6]

January 17: CDC posts interim guidance,[7] updated regularly in the coming weeks and months, for collecting, handling, and testing clinical specimens for the Novel Coronavirus, including biosafety guidelines for laboratories.[8]

January 18: CDC publishes interim guidance on how to care for Novel Coronavirus patients at home who do not require hospitalization.[9]

January 20: The Chinese government confirms human-to-human transmission of the virus.[10]

JANUARY 21: First U.S. Case Confirmed (from Travel)

January 21: CDC activates its Emergency Operations Center.

January 21: The Biomedical Advanced Research and Development Authority (BARDA, part of the Office of the Assistant Secretary for Preparedness and Response, or ASPR) begins holding market research calls with industry leading diagnostics companies to gauge their interest in developing diagnostics for the Novel Coronavirus and to encourage initiating development activities.

January 21: CDC holds its second telebriefing on the virus, with officials from Washington State, to discuss the first U.S. case, and Dr. Messonnier, who notes "CDC has been proactively preparing for an introduction of the virus here" and that a CDC team was deployed to Washington.[11]

January 21: CDC posts interim guidance, updated regularly in the coming months, on how to prevent the spread of the Novel Coronavirus in homes and other settings.[12]

January 21: Secretary Azar discusses Coronavirus with Lou Dobbs on Fox Business Network, noting "we have been heavily engaged at the outset" of the outbreak, with the CDC and the rest of HHS working under the president's direction to develop testing and alert health care providers.[13]

January 22: Secretary Azar signs a memorandum from CDC Director Redfield determining that the Novel Coronavirus could imminently become an infectious disease emergency, which allows HHS to send a request to the Office of Management and Budget to access $105 million from the Infectious Disease Rapid Response Reserve Fund.

January 22: FDA, working with test developers, shares an authorization application template with a diagnostic test developer for the first time.

January 22: ASPR stands up an interagency diagnostics working group with BARDA, CDC, FDA, NIH, and the Department of Defense (DOD).

January 22: HHS's Office of Refugee Resettlement began flagging any children referred from China for risk assessments and, if indicated by their travel and exposure history, for quarantine for up to fourteen days before being placed in the general community of the shelter. Screenings expanded to children referred from Iran, Italy, Japan, and South Korea on March 2.

JANUARY 22: All Outbound Trains and Flights from Wuhan Canceled[14]

January 23: ASPR convenes a Disaster Leadership Group (DLG), to align government-wide partners regarding the outbreak situation, communications strategies, and the potential medical countermeasure pipeline. The same week, conversations begin with manufacturers of N95 masks, enabling mask production on U.S. soil to rise from about 250 million a year in January to about 640 million a year in March.

January 24: ASPR forms three government-wide task forces—on health care system capacity and resilience, development of medical countermeasures (diagnostics, therapeutics, and vaccines), and supply chains—as part of work under Emergency Support Function 8 of the National Response Framework.

January 24: CDC hosts its third telebriefing on the virus, with Dr. Nancy Messonnier and officials from Illinois, where CDC has deployed a team to respond to the second U.S. case, from travel. Dr. Messonnier notes, "We are expecting more cases in the U.S., and we are likely going to see some cases among close contacts of travelers and human to human transmission."[15]

January 24: CDC publicly posts its assay for the Novel Coronavirus, allowing the global community to develop their own assays using the CDC design.

January 25: Five days before WHO's declaration of a public health emergency of international concern, Secretary Azar preemptively notifies Congress of his intent to use $105 million from the Infectious Disease Rapid Response Reserve Fund.

JANUARY 26: Five U.S. Cases Confirmed, All Travel-Related

January 26: ASPR holds first meetings of health care resilience, medical countermeasure development, and supply chain task forces, which continue several times a week or daily in the coming weeks.

January 27: In a Washington, D.C., speech, Secretary Azar shares that HHS is "proactively preparing for the arrival of the Novel Coronavirus on our shores," noting that "the Novel Coronavirus is a rapidly changing situation, and we are still learning about the virus." "While the virus poses a serious public health threat, the immediate risk to Americans is low at this time," Azar says, noting that he spoke on the morning of January 27 with China's minister of health and WHO Director-General Tedros Adhanom speak to discuss the Novel Coronavirus.[16]

January 27: CDC hosts a telebriefing with Dr. Nancy Messonnier, who notes that new travel recommendations are coming and that "there may be some disruptions" to Americans' lives as a result of the public health response, but that "this virus is not spreading in the community" in the U.S.[17]

January 27: CDC and State Department issue Level 3 "postpone or reconsider travel" warnings for all of China.

January 27: FDA begins providing updates about processes for approval and authorization to developers of vaccines, therapeutics, diagnostics, and other countermeasures for the Novel Coronavirus.[18]

January 27: CDC's Deputy Director for Infectious Diseases Jay Butler holds a call with the nation's governors on the Novel Coronavirus.

January 28: HHS hosts press briefing by Secretary Azar, Dr. Fauci, Director Redfield, and Dr. Messonnier. Azar says, "Americans should know that this is a potentially very serious public health threat, but, at this point, Americans should not worry for their own safety." He underscores, "This is a very fast-moving, constantly changing situation.... Part of the risk we face right now is that we don't yet know everything we need to know about this virus. But, I want to emphasize, that does not prevent us from preparing and responding."[19]

January 28: CDC posts interim guidance, updated regularly in the coming months, for airline crews regarding the Novel Coronavirus.[20]

January 29: The White House announces the establishment of the Coronavirus Task Force, which begins daily meetings.

January 29: CDC hosts a telebriefing with Dr. Messonnier, who notes that "despite an aggressive public health investigation to find new cases [in the U.S.], we have not."[21]

January 29: CDC posts infection prevention and control recommendations for Novel Coronavirus patients in health care settings, updated regularly in the coming months.

January 29: The Chinese government sends email to HHS acknowledging offer of U.S. expert assistance; HHS begins soliciting nominees for mission from across the department.[22]

January 29: ASPR, CDC, FDA, NIAID, and DOD host a listening session with industry—1,468 participants—on medical countermeasure development, health system preparedness, supply resilience, and medical surge needs.

January 29: The first repatriation flight from Wuhan, China, arrives at March Air Reserve Base in California, beginning the safe repatriation of Americans and marking the first use of federal quarantine power in more than fifty years. The operation eventually totals more than three thousand repatriations, with citizens from Wuhan and passengers from cruise ships. Repatriated Americans praise the work of the quarantine teams—including a couple who spent an extended honeymoon at Lackland Air Force Base in Texas.[23]

JANUARY 30: Sixth and Seventh Cases Confirmed in the U.S., Close Contacts of Travel-Related Cases

January 30: CDC hosts a telebriefing with Director Redfield, Dr. Messonnier, and officials from Illinois, where a sixth case is identified in a spouse of a confirmed case who had traveled to China. Director Redfield notes that most cases around the world outside of China are close contacts of travelers, and "the full picture of how easy and how sustainable this virus can spread is unclear."[24] (A seventh case is identified later that evening.)[25]

January 30: Department of State issues Level 4 warning, "do not travel," for all of mainland China.

January 30: The Trump administration hosts a call with Secretary Azar, Director Redfield, Dr. Fauci, and others with the nation's governors to present the administration's action plan on responding to the outbreak.

January 30: In an appearance on Fox News, Secretary Azar notes that, whether the WHO declares a public health emergency of international concern (declared January 31), "That doesn't change anything about what we are doing here in the United States...The president is ensuring that we are proactively preparing and also taking the necessary steps to prevent or mitigate any potential further spread here in the United States."[26]

January 30: Trump administration budget officials begin discussions about funding needed for development of vaccines and therapeutics, purchases of personal protective equipment for the Strategic National Stockpile, surveillance and testing, and state and local support.

January 30: ASPR launches a Coronavirus portal to receive market research packages and meeting requests from industry stakeholders interested in developing or manufacturing medical countermeasures.

January 31: At the recommendation of his public health officials, President Trump issues historic restrictions on travel from Hubei and mainland China, effective February 2.

January 31: Secretary Azar signs a declaration of a nationwide Public Health Emergency, which allows HHS to begin using a range of emergency authorities and flexibilities, and, together with other subsequent declarations, would allow emergency flexibilities for health care providers.[27] At a White House briefing, he notes, "The risk of infection for Americans remains low, and with these and our previous actions, we are working to keep the risk low. It is likely that we will continue to see more cases in the United States in the coming days and weeks, including some limited person-to-person transmission."[28]

January 31: CDC hosts a telebriefing with Dr. Messonnier, who notes possible reports of asymptomatic transmission and says, "We are preparing as if this were the next pandemic, but we are hopeful still that this is not and will not be the case."

January 31: FDA holds a virtual meeting with American Clinical Laboratory Association about the emergency use authorization application process.

Before breaking down the most important of these events that took place in January—in fact all of them were—it's useful to understand exactly how I obtained the documents to begin with. It started with a phone call from newly minted head of communications Assistant Secretary of the Department of Health and Human Services for Public Affairs Michael Caputo. He had been brought on in April 2020 to clean up what had been a messy messaging response from the agency and from the White House in general.

I met Caputo while covering the 2016 GOP primary for the New York 11th congressional district. It was a feisty race between the incumbent, the rather dull but steady Dan Donovan, and Michael Grimm the fiery former holder of the seat who had resigned a few years earlier and served jail time for twenty federal crimes. Political junkies might recall the square-jawed Grimm as the guy who threatened to throw a

NY1 reporter off the Capitol rotunda balcony and "break [him]…like a boy."

Caputo was doing some comms for Boy-Breaker Grimm, who though he eventually lost was still pretty popular in the district because, well, Staten Island. We got on and he kept in touch after that, so I wasn't totally shocked when he rang me shortly after taking over the messaging at HHS.

It seems the *Wall Street Journal* had done an interview with his principal, HHS Secretary Alex Azar, and he caught wind they were going to run a piece that badly misrepresented the facts of that interview. Did I want to run something refuting it, he asked. And of course I did. A day or so later, I had the transcript of the interview and some supporting materials. The report on the interview wasn't great; the *Journal* news side, unlike its opinion page, has often fallen into a don't believe the Trump administration for the sake of not believing the Trump administration mentality, but one of the support materials really knocked my socks off. You just read it.

I called Caputo and asked how much of the list, which I had obtained off the record, I could use in the piece. "You know this makes your guy look really good, right?" I spoke. "I mean, nobody knows any of this; everyone thinks they were just sitting on their hands for two months" There was a pause. Then he said, "What the hell, use it all." So I did.

Again, at the time, the going narrative in the news media and among Democrats was that January and February were wasted months, that the administration had done little if anything, or even worse, downplayed the virus while it festered. This document just blew that narrative out of the water. This was an enormous and important flurry of activity, especially considering that it all starts before China had even admitted it had suffered a single death. But unfortunately, this robust response from the administration was not communicated effectively by the White House to the American people. Why not?

The answer to this question strikes at the very core of the entire Donald Trump phenomenon. Shortly after he was elected in 2016, I asked a friend who was a comms operative for the GOP if he would work in the Trump White House if asked. He said he wouldn't; he actually used, shall we say, a more colorful phrase because he worried it would put him in compromising positions that could hurt his future career. When it comes to doing communications work for Donald Trump, there is one word that pretty much sums it up. That word is impossible.

The backbone of a political communications operation is message discipline. The principal, or the politician being represented, has to be willing to keep their remarks within constrained and controllable limitations. When it comes to

Donald Trump, that is just not a thing that can be accomplished for more than a few hours at a time. At every moment, he operated based on his instincts, and hey, the guy did become president of the United States doing it. But for the comms team, it meant being in a constant state of reaction. Forming a well-laid-out messaging plan for even a week at a time is just pointless.

An important and very telling example of the communications challenge the president faced given the hyperbolic style of his rhetoric came very early on in the crisis. On March 10, he appeared on Sean Hannity's prime time television show to discuss the virus. He told Hannity that he had a hunch, based on conversations he had, that the WHO was wrong about the fatality rate of the virus being 3 or 4 percent. That number would have meant the potential of millions upon millions of deaths. Trump said he believed the number was much lower, perhaps as low as .5 percent.

This was the occasion of the very first column I wrote about the pandemic, and I wasn't the only one who found the president's use of the word "hunch" to be problematic. When dealing with a public health crisis, you don't go around saying, "Hey, I have a hunch that maybe X, Y, Z." More than ever, the situation requires precise language of the sort you would hear from a doctor or scientist. It created the impression that the president was not taking this as seriously as was warranted, and the media, myself included, pounced on it. My goal was not to knock the president, but rather to suggest that Mike Pence, the head by then of the White House task force, who I describe as so measured you could tailor a suit by him, be the front-and-center voice of the response instead of Trump.

I still think that would have been wise, but here's the thing. The president was not wrong about the fatality rate; in fact he was pretty much spot-on. Months later, when I would interview Dr. Moncef Slaoui, who was by that time the head of Operation Warp Speed, this would be confirmed to me. In part because of the president's imprecise language, but also because of the news media's kneejerk reaction to doubt anything Trump said, information that turned out to be accurate was dismissed as nonsense. It was not.

So how did this happen? How the WHO get the fatality rate so remarkably wrong? Trump also explained that to Hannity in the interview. He said that there are so many asymptomatic carriers who never get tested that it skews the rate much higher. Evidence for this position would emerge as early as April from a study in Santa Clara, California, conducted by Stanford professor Dr. Jay Bhattacharya. At the time of his study, there had been one thousand cases confirmed in the county. But when he conducted antibody tests he found that fifty thousand people had been infected by the virus. That resulted in a fatality rate of 0.2 percent.

Bhattacharya, who would go on to be a coauthor of the Great Barrington Declaration, says himself that the initial findings were controversial; however by October, 82 of these seroprevalence studies had been done around the globe and though there were minor differences by region, the median fatality rate of these studies was indeed also 0.2 percent. This leads to a vital question that we may never know the answer to. If we had known in early March that the fatality rate was so relatively low, would we have gone into lockdown? Even as late as April 13, CNN was reporting data from Johns Hopkins that put the US mortality rate at over 3 percent. Again, this error was based on a severe undercount of asymptomatic cases, but voices like Bhattacharya's that questioned, correctly as it turns out, this data was at best ignored, and at worst vilified.

Of the policies laid out above in the HHS timeline, arguably the most important and the one Trump would most often tout was his partial ban of travel from China. Opinions vary on how many lives the ban saved. Trump believes it was in the millions; others put the number significantly lower. Tactically, the fact that Trump placed so much emphasis on this one move may have been an error. You can see why he made that choice, though.

The travel ban was exactly the kind of move that Trump loves: an out-of-the-box, fairly extreme measure that others advise against. It reminded me of one of the most important things I ever heard someone say about Trump, an anecdote that I think I think predicted many of his successes and failures in the response to the Coronavirus.

It happened at the National Security Seminar at the Army War College in the summer of 2018. The Seminar is a weeklong event that caps off the one year of education that the War College offers mostly to majors and colonels who are heading into positions of significant command. People from all walks of life, farmers, businessmen, politicians, and yes, even journalists, are brought in to take part in the classroom setting. A big part of the idea is that these officers will find themselves in their new positions more likely to interact with civilian leaders, for us civilians, it is also a fascinating glimpse into how our national security apparatus operates.

The story I heard was from a former diplomat, on background, during one of the morning keynote address question and answer periods. This person had served in embassies during both the Obama and the Trump administrations, and was asked, roughly, "What happens when Trump tweets something that seems to run against current foreign policy? Do the phones blow up at the embassy? Do you have to try to explain it?"

I remember the diplomat laughing, and yes, that, as it turns out, is exactly what happened: confused diplomats from all over the world trying to get a line on what precisely is going on. But then the answer continued. Sometimes, we were told diplomacy could find itself circling in ruts, well-worn paths that most diplomats do not wish to stray from lest the balance of the status quo be upset. Trump, the diplomat argued, was able to shake things up in such a way that new solutions to old problems could emerge. It is a tool that Trump used on many issues, perhaps most importantly his Middle East Peace efforts, but also in his approach to vaccines for Covid. When almost everyone, including medical experts from Dr. Anthony Fauci to Bill Nye the Science Guy, said a vaccine would take at least a year to develop, Trump didn't believe it. He thought with sufficient resources and enough cutting of red tape, a vaccine much sooner was possible. He was widely derided as spouting off antiscience gobbledygook.

We can look at the travel ban in much the same way. Trump wanted to act; that was the bottom line. An usual, he wanted to do something big and bold. And it was a risk: after all, on January 29 when the ban went into effect, there was no clear consensus that the virus was going to be a big problem, and that would remain the case for another month. The response from Joe Biden, who was not yet the presumptive nominee, would remain an issue for the rest of the lockdown, and eventually a big campaign issue, though it should have been a much bigger one. The day after the ban went into effect, Biden tweeted the following: "We are in the midst of a crisis with the coronavirus. We need to lead the way with science—not Donald Trump's record of hysteria, xenophobia, and fearmongering. He is the worst possible person to lead our country through a global health emergency."

Now this is very careful language indeed. Was Joe Biden specifically calling the travel ban xenophobic? He probably left himself enough wiggle room to say that he wasn't, which is exactly what his defenders would later argue, and yet at the same time, the tweet does appear to be directly addressing the travel ban, so the use of xenophobic would seem to be associated with that policy. But there is something else interesting about the tweet. We wouldn't know this until the fall when Bob Woodward's book on Trump came out, but earlier in the month of January and over the next several weeks, the Watergate veteran had interviewed Trump and two conflicting issues arose from it. On the one hand, Trump said that the virus was airborne and that it could be very bad; on the other, he said that he wanted to remain calm and not cause a panic.

The fact that Biden would accuse Trump of "fearmongering" at the end of January is telling. Biden, it seems, was also very aware of the need to balance a healthy

43

fear of the virus with a message that avoided panic. That is, of course, perfectly reasonable and rational, but during an election year, Biden would soon forget about his own worries regarding the spread of fear and go all in on a fairly absurd idea that Trump had blatantly misled the nation; after all, if he did, then so did Fauci when he said in late February that nobody should be changing their behavior.

The communications problems ran deeper than Trump's quirks though. An April 5 AP story shows us how. The headline of that piece was "US Wasted Months Before Preparing for Coronavirus Pandemic." The term "wasted" comes from a quote from Obama administration HHS secretary Kathleen Selbelius. The basis for this reported news piece, not an opinion piece, mind you, came in the second paragraph, in which the author Michael Biesecker wrote, "A review of federal purchasing contracts by the Associated Press shows federal agencies largely waited until mid-March to begin placing bulk orders of N95 respirator masks, mechanical ventilators, and other equipment needed by frontline health care workers."

That needs to be broken down a bit, but a key aspect of the piece is that HHS declined to comment for the article. That is simply insane malpractice. The list of administration actions above clearly shows that funds were being shaken loose and planning was underway to increase hospital preparedness as early as mid-to-late January. The willingness of news media outlets like the AP to frame the entire build up to the lockdown as "wasted months," along with the administration's bizarre failure to set that record straight created one of many narratives that would come to dominate the story of the lockdown and virus but which in fact had little relationship to reality. It should have been by no means surprising that the execution of purchasing contracts for medical supplies did not happen until the extent of the crisis was known, which was mid-March. The CDC would not even advise Americans to wear masks until April 3. The WHO would not issue such guidance until June.

One way that that we know the "wasted months" narrative was always nonsense is that the "we should have done much more in January and February" argument has all but disappeared: nobody really makes any argument for it; in fact, it is simply accepted false wisdom. In July, Joe Biden's campaign put out a five-minute ad detailing how he would have handled the virus differently and better. Ron Klain, who headed up the Obama administration's Ebola response, appears in the video in front of a chart showing what he alleges are the Trump administration's missteps. Amazingly, the chart begins in March. January and February are nowhere to be found. It's shocking. The very people who happily lied about Trump doing nothing in the early stages of the crisis didn't even try to argue that they would have done better. In fact, especially given that Biden was far less likely to ban travel from China, they almost certainly would have done far worse.

What the Biden camp realized that the AP and various other outlets paid no attention to was that nobody, certainly not Joe Biden, was calling for some massive surge in medical supplies during the months in question. Even as late as early March, prominent Democrats such as Speaker of the House Nancy Pelosi and New York City Mayor Bill de Blasio were urging Americans not to overreact and even to attend large gatherings. To suggest that they, or anyone else, should have had the foresight to start producing millions of masks at a time when masking was not even the protocol for the general public is stuff and nonsense. This is made even clearer by the fact that the Biden ad does mention that he would have surged personal protective equipment (PPE) production, but said he would have done so in mid-March, which is not only exactly what the Trump administration did, it is what the AP criticized it for.

This would be a recurring theme throughout the lockdown: the news media would seize on a half-baked story, run with it for days, sometimes weeks at a time, and then instead of ever saying, "Hey, looks like we had that one wrong," they would simply memory hole it, pretending it never happened. We saw this with ventilators and hospital beds. When the Army built a hospital at the Jacob Javits center in New York and sent the *USNS Comfort* hospital ship to the city, those facilities were barely used. But in the weeks leading up to their deployment, the narrative was that Trump wasn't doing enough. It was a tripling down on transparent lies behind a veil of trusting the experts and the science.

Over time, these stories that turned out to be basically flat-out wrong metastasized into an overall take. Even when the stories proved false, as was the case with alleged massive shortages of ventilators, the media would simply drop it with no correction and move on, creating the illusion that it was all still true. Trump himself would point this out as March drifted into April, boasting about the very real massive uptick in ventilator production. And what did he say about it? He accurately pointed out that all of the sudden, a news media that could speak of nothing but ventilators had absolutely nothing to say about them anymore.

A breathless *Washington Post* article on March 30, for example, again a "news" piece, excoriated Trump for saying that Gov. Andrew Cuomo did not need the forty thousand ventilators he was requesting. The piece contains quote after quote of experts and politicians mystified that Trump could even suggest such a thing. Included was this quip, "Some critics, like Patrick Chovanec, chief strategist at the investment advisory firm Silvercrest Asset Management, sarcastically noted they could only hope for the president to be right. "I mean, if we hand out too many ventilators, people might prefer it to breathing on their own," said Chovanec, who previously worked for GOP leaders on Capitol Hill.[29]

About two weeks later on April 17, Kyle Smith made clear in a *National Review* piece that the desperately feared shortages did not occur and—gasp—Trump, it turned out, was right. He wrote that, "on April 6, Cuomo noted, 'We're ok, and we have some in reserve.'" That was just seven days after the piece in the *Washington Post* appeared. A clear cycle was emerging, the corporate media would set its hair on fire over some allegation that Trump was neglecting the crisis, it would turn out not to be true, they would forget about it and move on to the next outrage, rinse and repeat.

Among the myriad steps and actions laid out in the HHS document, I obtained two that stood out.

January 9: CDC and FDA begin collaborating on a diagnostic test for the Novel Coronavirus.

January 10: China shares viral sequence, allowing NIH scientists to begin work on a vaccine that evening.

***

The development of testing would have some hiccups; science, as we were all to learn soon, is not exact, but these early efforts would eventually blossom into robust testing capacity that outstripped other nations. Likewise, the search for a vaccine was on, again before China had reported a single death, before the WHO would acknowledge that the disease was transmitted from human to human. By May, that effort would transform into Operation Warp Speed, organized by the president's son-in-law Jared Kushner, but honestly, HHS and the CDC would never truly get credit for beginning this fight so early.

***

Trump's balanced approach to the virus in those early days and his attempt to keep the country and the markets calm while his administration moved rapidly to prepare a response backfired, at least politically. In September, Trump would, not surprisingly, tell *Fox & Friends* that he gives himself an A+ for his response to the virus, but added, tellingly, "...other than public relations, but that's because I have fake news. On public relations, I give myself a D." He was right about the grade, but it wasn't all because of fake news: it was him; it was a White House that could not stick to the message; it was a president who said bizarre things about how soon we would have zero cases, and how the virus would magically disappear.

The downfall of the great communicator would be his failure to communicate.

***

In writing this book, I knew it would be important to talk to Fox News anchor Tucker Carlson. His show was conspicuous both for being extremely early in reporting about the potential danger of the pandemic, even back in January, but also being very early to question the efficacy of the lockdowns. I was curious if in meetings with his staff and producers similar discussions were happening, and to some extent, if similar mistakes were being made. In October, I conducted a fairly extensive interview with him, and this is what he had to say about these early days.

"You guys, even in January and February, you guys were raising an alarm about this when the *New York Times* was saying, 'You know, we're super prepared for this.' What did you guys see that others missed? I mean, what? Why? How were you ahead of that curve?"

"Well, we were just, I mean, it wasn't extraordinary prescience on our part. It was two things. 1) We were just more open to foreign stories than most other news outlets. I mean, there's very little coverage of the rest of the world anywhere in the United States. It's never been more parochial, the country, in my opinion, and never been more inward looking and narcissistic and sort of tiresome. And so our only advantage really in this was, I'm kind of interested in the rest of the world. I'm no expert, but, you know, my dad was a diplomat and we traveled a lot, and I, you know, I'm just interested. We put more stories of other countries on the air in general than most cable shows, I just read that stuff and so do a couple of my producers, so that was the first part. We're just more interested."

This seems like fair criticism of our media environment and the general attitude of the American people toward the rest of the world, but in fairness, we have a pretty big country here. But Tucker went on.

"...the second part, I think we're more skeptical of China, of its motives, of its plans, and certainly of its explanations. We just weren't instinctively willing to take their explanations at face value; we were much more skeptical because all people ought to be—it doesn't mean China's always lying. Sometimes they're telling the truth, but they do lie. And so you can't treat proclamations from the Chinese Central Committee the way that you would some press release from the Swiss canton they are just different. They lie a lot. So we were skeptical. That's it.

"And it came out of his wet market and from a pangolin or perhaps the horseshoe bat. It wasn't clear, but they're eating these weird animals that they shouldn't be eating and therefore it spread. That was our take on it. And the second you say something like that, you're racist and that really was kind of the sum total of the response to the story for weeks, anyone who mentions the origins of this is attacking Asians or something."

This point seemed important to me so I pressed it.

"Yeah, that is strange. I wrote about that, and they seem like, I really looked hard for evidence that there were attacks going on like they were claiming, and I really couldn't find any."

"Of course not, of course not." Tucker replied, "There is quite a bit of violence against Asian Americans, but almost none of it comes from right wingers. You know, I dare you to write that story. But anyway, please quote me because it's true. The uniform crime reports spell it out."

"So, when it hit, right? Like I remember having our Monday meeting our Monday meetings at the *Federalist* during the month of February. And really it was Bedford and Mollie Hemingway who were the two people who were like, 'Hey, this could be a thing.' And I remember sitting there thinking like, alright, you know, like SARS, whatever. No big deal. So it hits, right, and now it's like I got it. My kid's not going to school, New York City is getting shut down. And then the conversations really turned to how do we cover this responsibly? Were those conversations that you and your producers were having? I guess it's just that responsibility, like whether skepticism could be allowed. I'll be honest. I think we dropped the ball a little bit in the first month of just not being, not asking tough questions because we were honestly afraid that people could die if they didn't take it seriously."

Turns out it wasn't just us at the *Federalist*.

"Of course. I mean, I think that we dropped the ball in a lot of ways. I mean, in many ways, and some of those were the fault of the Trump administration. I mean, they understood right away that this, you know, exposed the vulnerabilities of our supply chains and of our offshoring of critical manufacturing, and that they didn't really do anything about it. So OK, that's one problem. Another problem was and this is a distinctly American problem. There was this predictable oscillation between, you know, kinda ignoring it and panicking over it. And there's always got to be a better alternative, you know, than being completely passive or having your hair on fire like that; I don't think they found that that spot soon enough.

"The bottom line is we are, at least my perspective on this, just running the show was for the first number of weeks. It was, you know, we should alert people that this could be a serious problem and that it could come west. And then once it arrived, you know, we didn't know the parameters of it. We didn't know really much about it, and it seemed like it could be really scary. Some of the numbers that international health organizations were putting out, we were terrified. Six percent death rate or something. Universal infections. I mean, those are big numbers.

"And then comes the comms team and the first couple of, the first two months was just their head was spinning. I think they got better eventually at getting the message out.

"I mean, part of it is, they were thinking political terms, too, and I know that because I talked to them, them being Trump and Pence, in mid-March, as this was gaining steam and it was clear to me that there, you know that they weren't really on it. And so I went and talked to Trump about it down in Florida. And, um and they were, you know, I think wanted to do the right thing for sure. But they were also, you know, ever aware that this is an election year. I mean, I do think, and I blame the Left overwhelmingly, for the ways we mismanaged this, but I think if I'm being as fair as I can be the fact that this took place in an election year, it made it far messier than it needed to be. I mean, it's very hard to think clearly about anything in an election year, particularly this year.

"And also I think Republicans who in general are kind of earnest people, not all. You know, Roger Stone's not earnest, but most Republicans are kind of, you know, they buy into the system, and, and they believe that reflects our values. They were very slow to pick up on the other ruthlessness of some Democratic leaders like Phil Murphy in New Jersey or Gretchen Whitmer in Michigan. I mean, these are people who weren't really that interested in approaching this as a medical crisis. They were immediately maximizing the political opportunities, like immediately, didn't even hesitate, and so I think a lot of Republicans were like that can't really be happening. I mean, this is a public health problem, so of course, we're gonna let the science guide us. And it was just too shocking. They couldn't metabolize what they were seeing until it was too late."

Chapter 3

<hr>

Myth 2—We Are All in This Together

In the fall of 2018, I spent two and a half days in Tokyo. This is not something I recommend anyone do. Sixteen-hour flights each way to spend about sixty-five hours in Japan with your time zone flipped on its head is a hard dollar. On the upside, it was a corporate junket so I flew first class, which let me get drunk on expensive booze and sleep in a flat bed on the plane that fit my 6'2" frame, but it was still just a crazy whirlwind.

There was one moment that stood out. I didn't have a lot of downtime, but one morning before interviewing the CEO of Philip Morris, I walked over to the Imperial Palace. My jaunt took me close by the old Tokyo train station, a lovely structure of dark red brick like so many in our Philadelphias and Baltimores. I came to a little two-lane, two-way empty street. On both sides, crowds of about thirty people were waiting for the light to change to a walk sign. And waiting, and waiting.

I was right on the curb with a clear path of vision down the pencil flat street. There wasn't a car even remotely in sight. The New Yorker in me started getting agitated. "Are we seriously doing this?" I asked myself. Yes. Yes, we were. In Gotham, if a sufficient gaggle bubbles up on a corner, we don't even wait for a yellow light: if there is a break in traffic, the herd moves. It's like a Manifest Destiny of the intersection.

I almost went. I wanted to show them that it was possible. That we are free people and if the intersection is empty, we can damn well make our own decision to cross the street. But I was already smoking a cigarette, which is illegal outdoors in public; several times, very polite police on bikes rode up and smiled to let me know to put out my smoke. I played dumb, even though "no smoking" signs abounded, but foreigners generally have such a low opinion of American intelligence, a big advantage in travel, that they just let me go. I decided not to press my luck and waited the approximately two weeks until the light changed.

I bring this up because there was, and still is, a lot of talk about how America, and especially New York City, should have been more like Japan or Singapore or something. Let's be clear. That was never going to happen. In those places, the state can say, "Don't leave your house, always wear a mask, and don't give hugs or have parties." And the people listen and—dare I even say—obey. In New York City, OBEY is nothing more than a trendy fashion designer, not a thing anyone actually does.

On March 11, two cases of the Chinese virus were detected in Monsey, New York, just north of the city in Rockland County. It is an Orthodox Jewish enclave and the second touch point of the Orthodox Jews with the virus; by then, we also knew that the man at CPAC with the disease was an Orthodox Jew who had been at the Shabbat dinner. In fact, one of Libby's coworkers had been at the dinner, which put her one step removed from an infected person, and our ten-year-old son Charlie and I two steps removed. We didn't really have a good idea of what contact tracing was at the time, but with the exception of seeing Libby and Charlie, I was already mostly self-quarantining and would be for several more weeks.

What ensued over the next few days in Monsey was a kind of voluntary series of checkpoints; to try to manage who was going in and out of the area, residents were encouraged to stay indoors, and staples were mainly delivered in the area. At this point, there was a real opportunity to do testing and tracing, a concept that we would continue to hear about for months. Testing and tracing really work only at this point in viral spread. Once the pathogen makes its way more broadly through the population, tracing programs become essentially impossible, especially with a population that has an independent streak.

It is also possible that by that time, owing to a dearth of testing, that the virus was already so widespread that tracing would already have been a dubious proposition. By December, we would know that scientists at the CDC had found traces of Covid from US blood donations in December of 2019. It was generally assumed in February and March that we were seeing the very first cases on the ground, but there was no real way to know that and over time the evidence suggested that the virus had arrived earlier. There were so many asymptomatic cases of the virus and the mortality rate among young healthy people was so low that we could have been swimming in the stuff for months by mid-March.

We simply did not have enough testing available at the time for a robust test and trace program, also the tracing program was not stood up and honestly never really would be. But more than that we now know that by the time of the Monsey two, the virus had been coursing through the city's subways, streets, and with eventual deadly effect, nursing homes for some time—likely weeks if not months.

Ultimately, in New York City, it would not be until December that we would have anything close to comprehensive contact tracing, and that was only after it was demanded by several local politicians and in an op ed I ran at the *New York Post.* That data showed that restaurants were responsible for just 1.4 percent of the spread of the virus, and yet on the very day the data was released, Gov. Cuomo shut down indoor dining for a second time. It leads to very real question of why we are wasting time and money on tracing if we don't trust or follow the science where it leads us. Restaurant workers began protesting in New York City; they most certainly did not feel like we were all in it together with them.

As with so much about what would become this pandemic, starting with CCP lies, we did not know enough to mount the response so many experts were calling for. Even if Gov. Andrew Cuomo and Mayor Bill de Blasio had decided then and there to shut down the city and environs, a move they would make about a week later, it's not clear New Yorkers would have obeyed; in fact, even as the death tolls would surge weeks later, many New Yorkers still, shall we say, adapted the "rules" to their own use, which is our way.

***

On March 15, New York City officially started to lock down. Schools would close, gatherings over fifty were banned, in-room dining and bars were shut down. By March 20, every nonessential business was shuttered. The main exceptions in

Gotham were grocery stores, pharmacies, takeout dining, ninety-nine-cent stores, and bodegas, which are the city's ubiquitous corner stores. Also, interestingly, liquor stores.

The fear really was the overwhelming sensation. It would not abate for some time. For the next several weeks—in fact, for nearly a month—the Coronavirus would be essentially a New York problem. Other places saw flashes of infection, but in America's largest and greatest city, we were clearly having a unique outbreak, one we would have to adapt to on the fly, but also one the rest of the nation would learn important lessons from. At the outset of the outbreak, the vast majority of the country was not in it together with New York City.

It is very important to understand and come to terms with just how fast everything happened. On March 2, de Blasio was still telling New Yorkers to go about their lives as normal; he was even giving mediocre movie recommendations to encourage business as usual. Five days later, five *days*, New York Gov. Andrew Cuomo would declare a state of emergency in New York State; about a week later, New York was starting to shut down. Everyone's heads were spinning. Fear was spiraling.

The speed that the lockdown train picked up in those first two weeks of March would become irresistible as the months went on. A central narrative began to emerge that told a story in which every other concern must take a back seat to stopping the spread of the virus. At first the measures seemed measured. The NBA halted play; Broadway went dark as Cuomo banned gatherings over five hundred. Although city and state officials wouldn't say it yet, most parents in New York City began preparing for the schools to close down.

It was already understood that school-age children were at very little risk of dying, or even becoming very sick, from the virus, which was a relief for parents and all Americans. Every death is of course a tragedy, but it is simply human nature to feel more powerfully the loss of a child than that of an elderly person, the latter being natural, the former being the snuffing out of a life not allowed to flourish. However, there were still concerns that asymptomatic school children could spread the disease. Over time, this risk would also be shown to be low and yet in the United States, unlike other nations, many schools would wind up closed for months on end.

I asked New York City Councilman Joe Borelli about the frantic first two weeks in March. As it turns out, our elected officials were almost as in the dark as we were. I wanted to know how much of a heads-up he and the others on the council had as announcements of closings and stay-at-home orders mounted.

"None, zero. And what you saw from other council members was just virtue signaling when they had as little idea as I did. They were interested in virtue signaling how we should all be at Chinese restaurants because some people were fearful that Chinese people would have the virus."

I then asked, "When the shutdown happened and the stay-at-home orders happened, from your perspective, it's between March 15 and the twentieth. Broadway goes dark, the restaurants are closed. About a week later, we get stay-at-home orders. What was your sense at that time as to how long this was going to last?"

"Maybe thirty days," he said.

"And what were you basing that on?"

"I was basing that on the decisions to build temporary hospitals because that would indicate that there would be some long-term need, right? Like, if it made sense to spend money and to spend ten, fifteen days building a hospital. Obviously, the need will probably last a month."

"And if I told you then, if I had said to you then five or six months later, we'd be in a very similar boat. Would you have been shocked?"

"Yeah, I would be completely stupefied."

What Borelli could not have understood at the time, what of none of us really could, was how hard it is to unring the bell of a lockdown. We understood that the effort was essentially based on flattening the curve and relieving pressure on hospitals, but in retrospect, it was almost inevitable that once those goals were reached, which really did happen in not much more than two or three weeks, more reasons to stay at home, to keep businesses closed, and to disrupt life in a million ways would emerge. It was like the public health version of the war in Afghanistan; nobody quite had a metric as to when the campaign could end. There was never a clear goal outlined.

Added to that issue was that state governments were handing almost limitless authority to governors and mayors to simply do whatever they wanted. Borelli, before joining the council, had served in the state assembly, so I asked him, "Since this went down—between five and six months ago, right?—how autocratic has the governance of the city and the state been compared to sort of normal operating procedures?"

"Well, I mean, for the governor, there is no check on his power. The state legislature, I think, voted twice to basically give emergency powers to the governor to make laws, and I mean, the way you're seeing them enforced is insane. If you read the [New York] Post coverage of the Joyce's Tavern debacle, I mean, these are people who are trying to even follow the rules and they got their liquor license suspended immediately...and she just got it back. And the State Liquor Authority basically was lying on camera. But it's just, like, it didn't even matter. They're enforcing the rules. The rule they were enforcing was serving a pregnant woman water inside while she waited for her outdoor table."

Borelli was referring to an incident in which a restaurant owner nearly lost her liquor license for allowing a pregnant woman to enter her establishment for a drink of water. This was obvious government abuse, but the larger point is that not only had Cuomo simply made this rule out of thin air, his enforcement mechanism was to take away liquor licenses; restaurant owners had no significant options to challenge the diktats of Cuomo.

What was so fascinating about talking to Joe was that his experience, and it is one that was common across the country, shows us how we fell into a kind of quicksand in our response to the Chinese virus. His understanding and the understanding of most people at the time was that we were handing governors and other executives an enormous amount of power for a very limited amount of time, to see us out of the immediate emergency. Perhaps the greatest failure of imagination that we suffered during the pandemic was in those early days of shutdown when almost nobody could have predicted we would be doing it for going months and months.

A big problem with operating under what basically amounted to a dictatorship by the governor was that it is extremely difficult for citizens to petition or protest a governor. If a few hundred restaurant owners and employees protest in Albany against Cuomo, it makes little difference. But if those same people are protesting outside the office of a state assemblyman, it does. Governors aren't really in the business of constituent services; the bottom line was that New Yorkers had little means of redressing Cuomo's whims.

***

One counterintuitive thing that was not really happening in New York City, but was in much of the rest of the nation, was the ransacking of grocery store shelves. As toilet paper became so scarce across America that using it as currency became the faddish joke, supplies in Gotham were pretty much fine. In general, grocery stores were fairly well stocked. This may just have to do with the way New Yorkers shop in general. Most people don't drive to the store and have very little storage space, so the once-a-week massive shop isn't all that common. A lot of New Yorkers go the store almost every day.

One exception in New York was hand sanitizer, which was hard to come by in early March, and which led to one of the more amusing moments of the early outbreak. At one of his first press conferences, that would soon become a counterpoint to the White House Task Force pressers, Gov. Cuomo announced that the New York State prisons had begun manufacturing hand sanitizer.

A few weeks later, *Vice* magazine, which since its founding in the late 1990s under Gavin McInnes among others has gone from being soft core porn for riders of the L train to something approaching an actual news outlet, would report that the prisoners weren't actually making hand sanitizer but simply repackaging already made hand sanitizer, despite Cuomo's claims that his product was not only safer but also smelled better than others on the market; he said it smelled of "lilac, hydrangea, and tulip."[30]

It was an early example of something that would occur and over again as the pandemic spread: jumping in with both feet as soon as possible on any idea that might help. That is a natural reaction to something like a deadly virus: do something, do anything. But, in fact, I'm not sure that anyone even saw a container of New York State hand sanitizer.

On March 14, Mayor Bill de Blasio announced that restaurants and bars in New York City would be takeout only. According to the *New York Post*, Hizzoner said, "Our lives are all changing in ways that were unimaginable just a week ago" in a statement released by City Hall, which acknowledged the step was "drastic."[31] Drastic indeed. It is difficult to describe what erasing nightlife actually means for a city like New York. Bars, dives, clubs, and the like are the living rooms of Gothamites. In New York State, nearly a million people work at restaurants alone. Although Washington State and Washington, DC had already issued such an order, this was a different order of magnitude. It was the beginning of a shutdown effort that would eventually lead to forty million job losses across the country. Suddenly all of this was very real.

But of course that reality was very different depending on whether you had a job that was shut down or one that you could perform from home. Not only would the economic impact on telecommuters be vastly smaller than that of those who flat out lost their jobs, many of the former would actually wind up in better shape financially. As far as the economic impact went, we were decidedly not all in it together.

New York City was creeping toward five thousand new cases a day by late March and would hit ten thousand cases on April 3. And this was with very limited testing capacity that was only targeting the sick. There was no way to know how many asymptomatic cases there were. And the deaths started coming in terrible waves, thousands a day. No place in the country would experience anything like it.

"Should I take Charlie to my mom's?" I was sitting in my backyard with my coffee, smoking a cigarette when Libby asked me that question over the phone. The idea had already occurred to me. My mother-in-law, Laura, of whom I have always been a big fan, lives in a charming little house on the beach in Long Beach Island, New Jersey. Nice big deck, nice big beach, nice big ocean. Libby and I knew what was coming for the city; neither of us wanted that for him.

If recollection serves, I did not hesitate in saying yes. It was an obvious choice. But that is not to say that I didn't have reservations. In his ten years on the planet, I think the longest I had ever gone without seeing my kid was two weeks. I knew the possibility, even the likelihood, was that this would stretch out far longer than that. A selfish instinct rose up within me; it didn't want to be denied the hugs and smiles, the guys' nights of pizza and chicken wings and hearing about his favorite video games. But I knew that in short order, my city was going to be no good place for a kid. And I counted myself lucky that Libby and I had the resources to send him off to bucolic beauty like a child whisked away from war-torn London during the German Blitz.

The decision was made remarkably quickly. By that afternoon, Laura was driving up to the city with her big dog to get my son. I walked the five South Brooklyn blocks across the BQE overpass to Libby's to say goodbye and help them get sorted. When I got there, Libby was packing food and supplies; as it turns out, she had been preparing for this for some time. She had a pantry full of dry goods that a Michigan Militiaman would be proud of. We put as much as we could in big bags and boxes, then she told me to feel free to ransack the rest, which I did over the ensuing weeks as I picked up her mail.

I don't remember how many times I told Charlie that everything was going to be OK. Almost certainly more than enough times to send a solid message that things were, in fact, not OK at all. He's a tough kid, but once the bags and boxes and supplies were loaded into Laura's minivan, it was time for them to leave. He hugged me and started to cry. I knew I couldn't, at least not yet. I think I winked at him, and told him he would have a grand adventure. Then the minivan slipped away, turning left onto 5th Avenue, and I was alone. For how long? I didn't know. Then I cried.

Walking back home was the first time I noticed there was no traffic. Just no cars on the street. Among the things I'd taken from Libby's apartment was a bottle of vodka and I poured a glass in my *Federalist* highball glass and sat in my yard. There was quiet, but not a good quiet, an eerie and chilling quiet most unnatural to the environs of Brooklyn. All I could hear was sirens. They were incessant.

I posted on Twitter about it, wondering if in fact there were more ambulances and cop cars bandying about than normal or if they were simply accentuated and made obvious by the general lack of any other traffic. My friend Karol Markowicz, a columnist at the *New York Post* who lives in Park Slop, was dubious, as is often her wont. She wasn't hearing them yet. But over the next few days, I think she did; in fact, everyone did. Looking back at the work of New York writers over these days, the sirens stand out; they pierced the sustained silence of the grinding halt.

At the time, neither Libby nor I had any doubt that sending Charlie down the shore was the right decision. Even a few months later, we were convinced of this. Today? Well, we're not so sure. And that is like a microcosm of everything that we have all been through. Decisions made in haste, better safe than sorry. I thought of James Joyce: in the particular one finds the universal, the great tragedy of the lockdown bears the scribe out.

This kind of thing was happening professionally too. Even before the official announcement of stay-at-home orders, some careful doubt was starting to creep in among my colleagues and I about the course the nation was about to undertake. Was this actually wise? We quietly wondered. We hinted at doubts. But like the entire country, we had to trust the science. Trust the science…It's science, man. Or as Bill

Murray once put it in Ghostbusters, "Back off, man, I'm a scientist."

But in the media, "pandemic correctness" was setting in. Part of us all being in it together, it turned out, was for us to accept without question what the leading or chosen scientists were telling us. Dr. Fauci and to a lesser extent, Dr. Birx, were becoming folk heroes, never to be doubted. And extremely well credentialed scientists who dared to question the lockdown measures were painted as obscure hacks on the fringe.

Dr. Jay Bhattacharya would describe it this way during remarks at Hillsdale College in early October. "When scientists have spoken up against the lockdown policy, there has been enormous pushback. 'You're endangering lives.' Science cannot operate in an environment like that. I don't know all the answers to Covid; no one does. Science ought to be able to clarify the answers. But science can't do its job in an environment where anyone who challenges the status quo gets shut down or cancelled."

That last word is an important one. Cancelled. It doesn't just imply that one's science, one's data, and one's conclusions are being ignored; it means that people believe one is acting in bad faith and should not be listened to on those grounds. Those scientists who questioned the most restrictive measures were accused of not showing sufficient deference to human life, It was a moral, not a scientific attack.

It was about this time that my boss Ben Domenech, patriarch of the *Federalist* started to be concerned. He was checking in regularly with our diaspora of staff all over the country, seeing if anyone needed anything. He also started a WhatsApp group of New York-based journalists. Over the next few months, it became a hub of information about what was going on. Few of us ever ventured out of our neighborhoods so it was good to get on the ground perspective from everywhere else. By "everywhere else," I obviously mean the rest of New York City. I mean, that's usually what we mean by everywhere else.

It was also informative to see how other journalists at the *New York Post* and *Commentary* and *Vice* were appraising the situation in secret. Behind the headlines and tabloid covers that insisted on a united front, nobody was very sure we were doing the right thing. What didn't occur to me until some time later was that we were complicit, along with the government, in not treating the American people like adults. Time and again, we wondered if it was responsible to tell the unvarnished truth or if we had to shape the news to ensure good behavior. Though we weren't scientists, a fact we were extremely cognizant and frequently reminded of, we were engaging in the same kind of groupthink that Dr. Bhattacharya was describing.

All that having been said, my recollection is that almost everyone was on board with the initial lockdown. Two weeks to flatten the curve sounded fair enough. The issue, and it was very real, was what we were seeing in Italy where hospital beds were running out as more and more people got sick. China's lies that had blinded us to the severity of the situation were being revealed as Europe, with accurate numbers, began telling the true tale of the Novel Coronavirus.

Initially, the lockdown was not so much meant to stop the spread of the virus as it was to ensure that medical capacity was not exceeded. This is inherent in the very term "flatten the curve." It's not "stop the curve," or "end the curve," it's "flatten it." At that time, we seemed to accept that the virus was going to run some course until there was a vaccine, and the job was to spread out the spread and make sure it didn't happen all at once.

As Monday, March 15, approached, the question of closing the schools was reaching a fever pitch over the weekend. Pretty much everyone wanted them to be closed, at least temporarily, but Mayor de Blasio was very reticent to do so. The teachers' unions were threatening to sue the city if schools didn't close, the *New York Post* editorial board wrote a scathing demand to close them, and it felt entirely unsustainable for the mayor to keep them open. I argued in the *Federalist* at the time that it made no sense to not at least close schools for a few days or a week until we knew more about the virus. After all, the school system had not used any snow days and the winter was almost over. Surely it was no trouble to keep kids home for a week; we literally would have done so for a blizzard, so why not for a pandemic?

The answer may well have had a lot to do with the teachers' union threatening the lawsuit. What de Blasio understood was that once the schools closed, he had no way of knowing when, or as it turned out if, kids would come back to finish the year. Once he decided that it was too dangerous to have schools open, he would later need to convince the union that it was safe to reopen. There was no way for him to know when that might be, so he knew if he pulled this trigger, he could be closing schools for the rest of the school year. And that was exactly what happened. And it wasn't just the kids who were about to have their schedules thrown into chaos.

Everyone I spoke to—over the phone or internet, of course—or read said that time was beginning to have no meaning. If you woke up at four in the morning you might as well stay up; if you sleep until noon, who cares? Life has a shape to it, a routine. Even for disorganized people, a pattern of activity punctuates the day and night, lets you know where you stand temporally; all of that was disappearing. Nobody knew what day it was because they were all the same. "Is it the weekend? Oh, I hadn't noticed."

On March 20, the shutdown turned into a stay-at-home order in both New York State and Illinois. Cuomo's executive order in New York would be called PAUSE for Policies Assure Uniform Safety for Everyone. It sounds a bit Orwellian, but it's actually too absurd and ridiculous to be given that description. There are two problems with the name, one with the abbreviation and one with the full phrase. The word pause suggests a momentary stop for a short period of time: you hit pause on a movie to check your email; you press stop because you are going to bed. Cuomo said on March 29 that he was extending the "pause" for two more weeks, and we were mostly dumb enough to believe it might end then.

The issue with the full phrase of the executive order was this idea of uniform safety was utopian gibberish. The problem with the concept of "uniform safety" or as the economist Glenn Loury would eventually put it to me in an interview; "perfect safety," was not only that it was impossible, but that people don't want it. Some people like to skydive or rock climb; others think that it's stupid and dangerous. For a government to ensure the safety or health of each citizen equally would require draconian and frankly unconstitutional laws. Now that is one thing for two weeks, but what about ten months?

When the two weeks passed and the "pause" did not abate a serious question began to emerge, when would it? A couple weeks of people out of work was one thing, a month, two months, or longer would cripple those thrust out of work without very seriously damaging, at least purely economically, those who could work from home. Political leaders urging the harsh restrictions were starting to gain a new ally in their effort to make Americans consent to the lockdown even without excessive enforcement, or frankly much enforcement at all. That ally was advertisers, and in the blink of an eye almost every thirty-second ad on television started to become a pro-lockdown public service announcement.

When we think about the media, we tend to think of TV shows, or news, or movies, but today it's advertising that has the broadest reach. This is owing to the explosion of content outlets across all platforms in the past two decades. The finale of *Seinfeld* in 1998 had nearly a fifty share in the ratings, which means half of the people watching TV were watching it. No sitcom in 2019 could even dream of reaching such numbers.

This has massive implications for how society views itself. We no longer watch the same stories; we are siloed into curated personal content bubbles. The machine knows what we like and gives us more of it; it gives our neighbor or the guy at the work water cooler an entirely different feed. No television shows or movies saturate the culture the way they once did, but ads do.

When, thanks to the grace of God, the Philadelphia Eagles won the Super Bowl in 2018, a key moment was a trick play called Philly Special. The team knew it as "Philly Philly," a reference to a series of Bud Light ads that used the phrase "Dilly Dilly." Everyone knew the ad because the ad is the only thing that pops up on everyone's unique feed across all our platforms.

The lockdown brought the dominance of corporate advertising into sharp and often deeply disturbing focus. It started with piano music. It wasn't exactly the same piano music in every ad, but it was kind of the same piano music in every ad. Shots of empty streets and first responders, various volunteers handing out supplies, families smiling at each other through screens, and then some message like "We're All In This Together."

Like so much about the pandemic, the single ad on its own was fine; the problem came when the next ad was another homage to lockdown, and the next, and the next. Most of these ads had little to do with showing the benefits of a product you could purchase; instead, they were selling the brand, offering up the compassion and caring nature of corporate America. And in the process, they were confirming the rightness of the lockdown.

It was remarkable to watch corporate groupthink develop so quickly and in real time. Corporations and ad agencies didn't have to get together to settle on a message any more than news organizations did. A "how to advertise in a pandemic" playbook was developed, focused on the unique nature of the moment and how the corporation could selflessly help. At the same time, this constant pitter-patter of lockdown vignettes played a big part in manufacturing consent to the lockdown. Ads are first and foremost aspirational; what we see is supposed to be what we want. And what we were meant to want, more or less the only thing we were meant to want, was compliance with the rules set by the experts and authorities to stop the spread of the virus.

Once we were a few weeks into the lockdown, it wasn't just the ubiquitous style of the Covid ads that happened, but also a shift in which companies were running ads. Internet companies, seeing a huge moment for their products in the stay-at-home situation, pounced. They were basically heroes, the powerful force keeping America going, and they weren't really wrong. There is a strong argument to be made that even twenty years ago, we did not have the technology or online capabilities needed to lock down in the way we did in 2020.

Placing such severe restrictions on who could leave their house and when would not merely have been the subject of debates over freedom. It would have been more or less impossible without the big tech solutions to telecommuting. In 1999, we did not live in a world where this kind of lockdown was even possible; today, we absolutely do.

But something interesting happened as the ads inundated our airwaves. People, a whole lot of people, just hated them. I can be included in that number. It's not really hard to see why. We had already spent two weeks trapped in our houses or apartments and were running out of Netflix shows to binge watch after for some reason, we all became obsessed with *Tiger King*. The last thing we needed was a reminder that we were in lockdown. Yeah, we get it. I remember thinking, I'm literally trying to watch TV and take my mind of it and you people have to throw it down my throat at thirty-second intervals all day long.

I spoke to Jim O'Neil, an ad exec at Arnold with about three decades of experience. I wanted to know how this all goes down, what the mechanics of these kinds of campaigns that play such a strong role in shaping public opinion consists of.

"So like it's March 15," I said to O'Neil, "This is all just starting. Is a client calling? Are you guys calling a client? How does this process start for an advertising agency and a corporation that want an ad like this?"

"I know this is a bad answer, but it depends. Many times, the agencies will spot trends and make recommendations to clients on how to respond to them. In a situation like this I'm sure it was both ways, almost simultaneously. I mean, when this thing hit, I was actually in Atlanta, visiting my mother in the second week of March, and when it came time to fly home five days after I got there, my wife said to me, 'I think you should stay. This thing is really turning into something. And I don't know if I want you getting on a plane and coming back here to us.' Now, I went out to dinner in Atlanta at a place called Bones, a steakhouse, with a buddy and his wife; they were celebrating their son's twenty-fifth wedding anniversary and the place was packed. I got back here and all the restaurants were closed. So it wasn't even. It wasn't an even distribution of reaction."

The New York that O'Neil stepped back into was already a ghost town, and even though much of the country had not yet locked down to that degree, the New York experience quickly became the lens through which the entire nation viewed the virus and the response to it. But I wanted more detail on the process. And O'Neil went on.

"So typically, what happens in a situation like that is somebody on the marketing team or somebody in a position of authority at the agency will spot these trends, make a recommendation to the client, or the client will call and say, 'You know, I think we need to respond to this in some way. How would you recommend that we react to it?' The wheels begin turning pretty quickly. And you can, in this day and age, you can crank out and ad in three days if you need to. Pretty professional looking, too."

"Working on the campaign generally requires anywhere from two months on the tight end to four to six months on the loose end to develop up a campaign. In this situation, Ford began running ads, I think it was as early as mid-March, probably about the time I was coming back from Atlanta. They were running ads talking about giving people grace period on their loans. Right? So they changed gears pretty quickly."

But how did all the ads wind up looking and feeling the same?

"So you mentioned something that I think everybody noticed, which was that they all kept using the same words they all kept using. The same piano music—it was as if every advertising agency got together and held some meeting about this is what the Coronavirus ad looks like. So clearly that didn't happen…"

"Well, I'm sorry to interrupt, but I think I think part of the reason is that it happened so quickly, that as I said, most agencies what I would call, quote unquote, real agencies, mainstream big agencies that handle big brands typically require sixty days just to put together a simple message. And the reason is because there's a lot of thinking that goes into what that message needs to be and should be. And in most cases, and of course, then they want to give the creative process time to develop, to flower and become something that is special. And you can't do that in a couple of weeks.

"When you get into a situation like this, I think everybody ends up saying basically the same thing because it's safe to a certain extent to do that. It's not a, quote unquote, creative development process or even, it's barely a strategic development process. But how did they know what that thing was in the first place? It was copycatting. I mean, just copycatting early. Somebody, a client, sees something that to them hit them. You're right from a totality perspective.

"And in circumstances like this, when there isn't really a creative development process or even much of a strategic development process, clients do tend to dictate the terms of what the expression is going to be. And they do that based on conversations with lawyers. They do it based on conversations with public relations communications specialists. And when they put together a brief for the agency and you're kind of balancing, as you know, Trump was trying to do and frankly, as the media was trying to do. I can tell you all of our meetings started and ended with the question of what is the responsible way to impart of this information, you know, that that was the first that was the first and the last question. And then outside of that, if you wanted to, you know, raise other issues. OK, now that began to change eventually, but that's certainly how it started."

"How did agencies balance that?" I asked. "It seems that they did at least a reasonably good job. I mean, the overall message seemed to be what it seemed to be was like, 'We'll get through this as a company and will do whatever we can to help'—was that sort of what everyone landed on?"

"Yeah. And then you have companies like Budweiser. And I believe this was a pretty smart thing for them to do, but they took the dollars they would have invested in sports marketing, and they redirected them to helping heroes on the front line. So, you know, they took all the money that they would have advertising for MLB and the NBA and they redirected them."

Just like the news media, and most of our political class, the nation's advertisers were taking no chances. The path of least resistance was followed. At least initially, this was simply corporations covering their own asses with the safest ads possible. But as the lockdowns persisted, some economic sectors such as Big Tech and large corporations with major delivery capacity would start to feel the boon. According to *Business Insider*, by October, billionaires had gained half a trillion dollars in wealth. For them, the new normal was becoming a cash cow even as it wiped small businesses off the map. That conflict of interest would grow more apparent as the shutdown wore on.

As the virus was taking hold in late March and much of America was coming to a standstill, we already knew that we were not all in this together. The lines were being drawn in bank accounts and mailboxes across America, where paychecks flowed or ebbed. With schools closed, single parents faced impossible childcare choices and the children a hapless experiment in remote online learning and the absence of the physical presence of their friends. Church communities could not gather even as big box stores and liquor marts profited on their cornered markets.

In the months that followed, time and again we would see our most arrogant pro-lockdown politicians like Nancy Pelosi, Gavin Newsom, Andrew Cuomo, and countless others flout their own restrictions. Unfairness is a bitter pill to swallow, but when it is clothed in self-righteousness, it becomes impossible to digest. But the most important aspect of the hypocrisy wasn't the hypocrisy at all. It was that when politicians place restrictions on the citizenry that run entirely counter to human—or at least American—nature, they are inevitably bound to violate them themselves. For those in power, it is always a free society

Chapter 4

◇

Myth 3—The Term "Chinese Virus" Is Racist

To get a sense of how quickly the Coronavirus became utterly politicized, we need look no further than its name. Yes, its name. On March 10, just days into what would become a disastrous and deadly period of lockdown for America, Rep. Grace Meng, vice chair of the Congressional Asian Pacific American Caucus, decided that her priority was not saving lives or jobs but rather calling people racist for using the term "Chinese virus" to refer to a virus that came from China.

This ridiculous sideshow of outrage would play out for months as those on the Left and almost all of the corporate media accepted this accusation of racism while conservatives and Donald Trump rolled their eyes at it and used the term, provoking a cycle of PC culture war. The reason that progressives gave for why the terms Chinese virus, China virus, or Wuhan virus were suddenly racist, even though they had been widely used for over a month, is that saying these things would cause people to commit acts of violence against people of Asian descent. Specific incidents of this were few and far between, but those pushing the theory used numbers they claimed pointed to an uptick in hate crimes against Asians and Asian Americans. In fact, there had been for several years an uptick in hate crime reports across all races. This was partially due to the relatively novel nature of "hate crimes" in our society and legal system.

A breathless article from *Psychology Today* had this to say about the president saying "Chinese virus:" "Racist words from the top lead to racist actions by those disinhibited by the president's rhetoric and dog whistles. Could they lead to actual war, and further actions against Asian Americans? Honestly, can you imagine Asian Americans feeling safe with words like this from the president?" I think we can all imagine Asian Americans feeling safe even though the president accurately states where the virus comes from. In fact, it seems highly likely that the vast majority of Asian Americans hadn't thought twice about it until progressives, ever intent to police our language, decided it was problematic.

The real reason, aside from the constant barrage of accusations of racism hurled daily at President Trump, had to do with critical race theory and intersectionality. The way we know that is both sides agreed that terms like German measles or Spanish flu were not racist. And frankly, it was remarkable just how quickly the term Chinese virus became racist. in January, the phrase had been tossed about the media landscape like peanuts at a baseball game with not so much as the Wuhan bat of an eye.

The accusation of racism was and is flat out absurd on its face. There was no intent by anyone to insult or attack Chinese people or any Asian people by using the term. What would the motive of such an attempt even have been? Who would have benefited from an increase in racism toward Asians? It simply makes no sense.

This was arguably the first overt politicization of the crisis. Prior to this controversy, Democrats and even some conservatives had been critical of Trump's tone on the issue, what else is new, and had also made vague statements about how we should be doing more, thought it was never quite clear what the more was. In general, though, there was really no issue surrounding the virus that divided Americans on clean party lines until the name controversy.

I found it very important to use the terms Chinese and Wuhan virus. My outlet, as well as the *Federalist*, created a "Wuhan Virus" tag and encouraged its use along with Coronavirus and Covid. The reason was that the CCP was not an unwitting victim, but rather a force that lied, mislead, and undermined the world's response to what would soon be a pandemic. My point, the *Federalist*'s point, and the president's point in using those terms was to forever tie the Chinese government to the time bomb they had unleashed.

And of course, the greatest beneficiary of the idea that saying Chinese virus is racist is the very CCP that gleefully supported the idea. Chinese propaganda worked overtime to try to downplay their role with catchy social media memes in which they insisted they had been straightforward and honest, and it was stupid Donald Trump who failed to heed their warnings or take their support. These were blatant lies; in fact, China refused to allow Americans and others access to much-needed information about the virus until it was much too late.

In terms of domestic politics, the die was cast. The Democrats were practically daring Trump and his allies to continue using the phrase and anyone who knows anything about the president knows that he would rather eat steak tartar without ketchup than back down from a fight, any fight, over political correctness. In significant ways, fighting political correctness was the raison d'être of his entire 2016 campaign. "PC culture is killing us," he would insist. And his entire presidency was a thumb in the eye of those who would decide what we can and cannot say.

This controversy also pointed to a divide that has been emerging between Left and Right in the United States. For the three years after the election, those opposed to Trump put their faith in the idea that he would be removed from office for Russian collusion. This, of course, did not happen, but it did cast Vladimir Putin's Russia as the prime geopolitical foe of the United States; in the fever dream-addled minds of the president's starkest enemies, Putin was already the puppet master controlling a sitting US president. This was remarkable given that in 2012, President Obama had mocked Mitt Romney at a debate for saying Russia was a threat; the Democrat said, "The 80s called; they want their foreign policy back."

Also during that time, the American Right was increasingly expressing ire at China. The stories about Uyghurs being held in concentration camps were gaining attention, the crackdown on Hong Kong filled pages of right-wing journals and occasioned a visit from Sen. Josh Hawley, a voice of growing power on the new Right. There had been tariffs, if not an all-out trade war with the Chinese, and their military threat was growing by the day. A new dividing line was being established, with the Left more forgiving of China and distrustful of Russia and the Right in the opposite position.

This is a vital advantage for the CCP in swaying American public opinion regarding whether they are a greater threat than Russia. Criticism of the Chinese government is racist while criticism of Russia is obviously not. Ironically, China now has a similar incentive to push the narrative of anti-Asian racism that the Soviet Union had regarding antiblack racism in the Cold War. The obvious and important difference is that antiblack racial inequality was very prominent in the 1950s and 1960s; Asians today face little discrimination in America, and in fact have higher average incomes and dominate our elite academic institutions. If this if horrible bigotry, it is the most generous bigotry in the world's history.

So this battle over the name of the virus was not merely petty politics or the puerile process of political correctness; it actually reflected a rather important new battleground in American politics. By the summer, intelligence reports would show that just like in 2016, there was foreign interference going on in the American presidential election of 2020, but this time with a twist. Although Russia once again was angling to defeat the Democrats, China was working to harm Trump's chances and help put Joe Biden in the White House.

This ridiculous fight over the name of the virus was not a good start to an effort by Americans to come together in a time of crisis and act as one. We could not even agree what to call the crisis. And like pretty much everything else in the America of 2020, race would play a central role again and again. Next to politics, nothing did more to hamper our response to the virus than our society's obsession with race. The virus might not have cared about race, but Americans did, and especially on the Left, the lens of race would continue to be a contributor to the contours and hues they saw in unfolding events. Eventually, this would become so stark as to be truly shocking.

For the president's part, he would never stop using the term "China virus." There were times when he laid off of it for a while, but it would always come back. Usually, this was just when he felt he needed to troll his opponents more

Chapter 5

⎯⎯◆⎯⎯

Myth 4—Trust the Science
and Wear Your Mask

What we couldn't know in March, but what has become painfully clear since then is that the magical incantation "Trust the science" is not nearly as efficacious as we then hoped. This was perhaps no place clearer than in the mask guidance. Until April 3, the CDC had insisted that members of the general public should not be wearing masks in public—to the extent that there was an "in public." By September 16, CDC director Robert Redfield would testify before Congress that masks were the best precaution against the virus, even better in some ways than a vaccine. How on earth could this reversal have happened?

It makes no sense to suggest that scientists had no knowledge of the potential benefit of masks. One of the earliest viral moments of the entire pandemic was drones in China admonishing citizens on the street to wear their masks; this was in January. In other countries, governments believed as the virus emerged more widely that masks helped and urged their use. So why didn't our government do the same? Ultimately, this is not only a question we still don't have the answer to, but also one we might never have the answer to. To confuse matters even more, despite Redfield's rather hyperbolic claims about the magic of masking, there is substantial disagreement in the scientific community to this day about how useful masks are.

If anything, this confusion over the ubiquitous face gear only grew as the US entered into a second winter spike in late November and early December. By that time, even without mandates everywhere, polling was showing that between 80 and 90 percent of people were wearing masks in accordance with the guidelines. So how did the spikes happen anyway? Would they have been worse without masks? All of this is still a matter of speculation.

As with so much of the tangled web of the Chinese virus response, the question of masks turned out to be a far more subjective one than the simple phrase "trust the science" could ever capture. First of all, as noted above, there were and are some scientists, although in the minority, who basically eschewed the wearing of masks altogether. But even among those who did favor mask wearing, exactly when and where they were needed was a point of serious contention. And this is exactly how the mask became one of the first the first major issues surrounding the virus to set Donald Trump up against

Joe Biden. The face mask would come to be the most visible and obvious difference in the way each man treated the virus.

By May, masking was moving from a recommendation to a mandate in many places and emerging as a symbol of just how fearful of the virus one was, and also of political affiliation. I wrote a piece for the *Federalist* arguing that the president should not wear a mask in public. The basic argument was that having the head of state wear one while representing our nation when he could be protected in other ways presented a poor image, one of defeat and resignation, not drive and fight.

The crux of the issue became setting a good example, which may be a lot of things but is not exactly a matter of science. The argument went that Trump should wear a mask whenever possible to show Americans that they should also wear masks. There are a few assumptions that underlie this position, but the most obvious and important is the assumption that huge swaths of people are going to do something just because they see the president did it. It's not that Trump doesn't have plenty of supporters who love him— he does—it's just that that love doesn't necessarily translate into mirroring his behavior. Trump doesn't drink, for example, but a lot of his supporters sure do.

And Trump, from the very beginning, was generally in favor of mask wearing and said so many, many times. But his approach to masks was, to be fair, more relaxed; he ultimately viewed it a personal choice, not something that government, certainly not the federal government, should regulate. Not surprisingly, most of the corporate media took Trump's nuanced approach to masking as the president mocking masks or denying their effectiveness, for there could only be two approaches in their mind, the right one and the wrong one, and by the way, Trump's was always the wrong one.

Biden would, of course, take another approach to masking—one that would mirror his campaign strategy of staying in the basement to avoid Covid or creating large crowds, not that he had shown any ability to draw large crowds, but as with so much about Coronavirus response, it was the thought that counted. A masked Biden would be a staple of campaign ads. He would often appear in situations where he was nowhere near anyone outside his immediate family and still be masked. He was exemplifying a kind of mask zealotry that would soon sweep much of the nation.

As a personal matter, Americans took to the masks in very different ways. For some, it became almost a point of pride, a way of showing solidarity and of doing one's part, which is understandable. And rather quickly, masks with fashion designs and sports logos and political messages and weird goofy clown mouths began to appear. For me, this was a line I was not willing to cross. I saw these "fun" masks as a kind of normalization of the practice and I began to worry rather early on that the masks might never come off. By late May, I was expressing this fear in a column for the *Federalist*, writing:

"When can we take off the masks? It's a simple enough question. Three months ago pretty much nobody outside of recent Asian immigrants in urban Chinatowns donned the face protectors, but now they are ubiquitous.... The emerging question is whether the changes are temporary and specific to this one threat, or if they will become permanent.

"After all, even if the virus disappeared tomorrow through some force of magic, face masks would still be an effective tool to slow the spread of other deadly diseases like the flu. If the philosophy is that changing our ways is worth it if it 'saves even one life,' then the end of this will be everyone wearing masks at baseball games and plays, in airplanes and shopping malls."

Sitting here in December, I still don't know the answer to the question of whether we will wear the masks forever. It's something I have tried specifically not to normalize in myself or my son, actually. He dutifully wears his mask in school, well, his learning pod, but the moment we are outside and distanced, I have him take it off. I sincerely do not want it to become a part of him.

One strange thing about the masks is something I noted to Chris Bedford at a hotel restaurant, having taken the elevator and walked through the lobby with my powder-blue covering, was that the more normal it became, the more surreal it became. That is to say that in the beginning, when we thought masks would only be used for a short time and we still forgot to put them on, or laughed at having to, it felt like some kind of weird inconvenience. Once it becomes a normalized practice, it is more like a dream you can't awake from. Do I now live in a world where I will never see the faces of most of the people I encounter each day? Like the ban on gathering in crowds, this felt like a deprivation of basic humanity.

By late summer, Dr. Fauci was addressing the issue by making two basic and somewhat contradictory arguments about it. First, he said that the data at the time did not back up enforcing mask compliance, and he also stated that there were concerns that the first responders and essential workers would run out of masks if the general public made a run on them. This had been expressed by the Surgeon General in a tweet in March, in which he begged people not to snatch up the needed PPE. These explanations are not entirely mutually exclusive, but they do raise some questions.

As to the idea that there would be some run on mask supplies leaving first responders in a lurch, this was a period of time when the guidance from the task force was that a scarf or bandana was sufficient. I myself bopped around with a yellow bandana that I happened to find in my apartment around my neck. So if the concern was medical mask shortages, why not tell people to wear a scarf? As to the efficacy of masks, it is still not entirely clear how the change in mask guidance actually came about. Curiously, in the United States, the guidance changed on April 3, while it would take the WHO until June 5 to recommend masks for people who can't socially distance, and only, or at least "especially," by the way, for people who can't socially distance.

On May 21, the *New England Journal of Medicine* published an article on the use of masks in hospitals that cast significant doubt on the effectiveness of masking outside of a hospital environment, writing that, "We know that wearing a mask outside health care facilities offers little, if any, protection from infection. Public health authorities define a significant exposure to COVID-19 as face-to-face contact within 6 feet with a patient with symptomatic COVID-19 that is sustained for at least a few minutes (and some say more than 10 minutes or even 30 minutes). The chance of catching COVID-19 from a passing interaction in a public space is therefore minimal. In many cases, the desire for widespread masking is a reflexive reaction to anxiety over the pandemic."

Reaction to the article was intense on both sides of the mask debate. Those who opposed universal masking mandates saw it, rightly, as justification for their position. The pandemically correct mask enthusiasts, on the other hand, were outraged at this supposedly irresponsible paragraph. This latter group's anger was sufficiently frightening to the authors that the next month, they wrote a letter clarifying their position, but in fact, the clarification did not change their position; here is part of it: "As the rest of the paragraph makes clear, we intended this statement to apply to passing encounters in public spaces, not sustained interactions within closed environments…A growing body of research shows that the risk of SARS-CoV-2 transmission is strongly correlated with the duration and intensity of contact: the risk of transmission among household members can be as high as 40%, whereas the risk of transmission from less intense and less sustained encounters is below 5%."

This was not a correction; they were absolutely not saying they had been wrong in stating that masks were of little use in passing encounters. But their clarification, aside from covering the authors' own asses, gave ammunition to fact checkers at outlets like *USA Today* to downplay the very important message that wearing masks outside when you can social distance is of barely any use. Meanwhile, governors, mayors, and the media were insisting that masks should be worn anytime one stepped out of one's abode without any scientific basis for it, and eventually in many places, this relatively useless display of face covering became a mandate.

A Danish study in November would also cast significant doubt on the efficacy of masks. In it, one group of Danes wore masks whenever they left the house and another group, the control group, did not. What they found was that 1.8 percent of the mask-wearing group caught the virus, while 2.1 percent of the control group did. Once again, much the scientific community and again including the authors of the study insisted that they still thought people should wear masks. OK. But then what really was the purpose of the study? Why was it that every time data pointed to bad news about the virus, it became instant gospel, but every time data made things look better, it was an outlier that shouldn't be given too much credence?

By December, the *New York Post* would report on a study that showed that wearing used masks could actually make one more susceptible to the virus: "Researchers from the University of Massachusetts Lowell and California Baptist University say that masks slow down airflow, making people more susceptible to breathing in particles—and a dirty face mask can't effectively filter out the tiniest of droplets. 'It is natural to think that wearing a mask, no matter new or old, should always be better than nothing,' said author Jinxiang Xi. 'Our results show that this belief is only true for particles larger than 5 micrometers, but not for fine particles smaller than 2.5 micrometers.'"

This was an issue that President Trump brought up, including at a presidential debate, and was widely mocked for. His point was that when people wear masks, they tend to touch them, take them off and put them on, reuse them, and in general, just treat masking in ways that reduced its efficacy. The science was on his side on this but it didn't matter. To the media, he was mocking mask wearing in a dangerous way; it was ridiculous, but that didn't stop the media from running with it.

All of this suggests that there was not then, and in fact never would be, a consensus in the scientific community about exactly when and where to wear masks. This led to a situation where for many people, mainly on the Left, wearing a mask even when the guidelines didn't call for it, like when you are outside and socially distanced was justified first as a measure that can't hurt, even if it didn't help, and second as a way of setting a general example. For others, mainly on the Right, wearing masks when they weren't called for appeared as useless virtue signaling and was a needless annoyance at best, and dehumanizing in the sense that it made us literally faceless at best.

To my way of thinking, this latter point got too short shrift. "It's just a mask" was a fine sentiment for a few weeks, but for months? Forever? It is not some minor thing for people to not be able to see each other's faces. It is a primary form of communication; it leads to coupling and mating, just as one can feel a crowd when they are in a crowd, they see the sea of faces, know where they are, and know who they are with.

One of the first times I found myself back in Manhattan in June, Libby and I took Charlie to the West Village. In Washington Square, there was life, music, people dancing. But on more than one occasion as we walked, not close to anyone, just walking, some person, usually a middle-aged white woman, would yell, "Mask!" at us. These kinds of confrontations were going on all over America, sometimes in hysterical viral videos. But it's an interesting and rare thing.

There are not a lot of situations in our society where people feel comfortable angrily scolding a stranger. One is actually smoking. Anyone with the habit can tell you stories about smoking outside and having people make faces, or say, "How can you do that?" Or call you disgusting. And it's not that your smoke, outside, feet away from a person, is putting them in harm's way, it's that it is an opportunity to express moral superiority. And because the smoker is acting in a bad way, the scold is justified in treating them rudely.

This was similar with the masks. The angry women weren't in danger—in fairness there were some men too—but they weren't being harmed; rather, they were lashing out at people for not showing deference to the virus, for not performing it. And like I said, this is really is pretty rare. Most of the time, when people are harming themselves and setting a bad example, people don't feel free to just harass them. Nobody walks up to a fat person eating a Big Mac and says, "What the hell is wrong with you? Can't you see you're obese?"

There was a similar phenomenon going on in social media. Some people's avatars on Twitter would be masked. When you step back and think about it, that is truly strange behavior. I mean, a photo of you can't infect someone if they look at it on the iPhone or laptop. It really is nothing more than signaling. One early iteration of this phenomenon in social media took place during the 2008 presidential election, when Facebook users put "Hussein" as their middle name to show support for Barack Obama, but importantly also to show a rejection of supposed racism against him. It is a signal to affinity groups with the bonus of giving one a smug sense of superiority.

Social media played an even more direct role in the mask question, among others. Companies like Facebook and Twitter began flagging and even sometimes censoring articles that questioned the efficacy of masks. This despite the fact that both before and after the pandemic began, there was a serious scientific debate about just how effective masks were. In fact, it's a debate that goes back a hundred years, when after the Spanish flu, some scientists came to the conclusions that masks, which were ubiquitous, were not efficacious.

As with so much about social media and its algorithms, it was never clear what standards their censorship was tied to. In October, Twitter would suspend the account of Dr. Scott Atlas, by then a lead voice on the White House Task Force. The tweet read, "...the right policy is @realdonaldtrump guideline: use masks for their intended purpose—when close to others, especially high risk. Otherwise social distance. No widespread mandates. #Commonsense." It was a quote tweet above a number of examples of scientific studies that supported his position.

So here we had a situation where a top government official was tweeting out CDC guidance and explaining the position with credible scientific studies but it was not only censored, the account itself was blocked. What exactly was Atlas in violation of? That was never made clear, even after his account was reinstated.

The myth of just trust the science was the most harmful of the pandemic. Not just because much of the science was being hidden, but because even when it emerged in public, if it did not fit the pro-lockdown narrative, it was simply ignored, as happened when Gov. Cuomo closed indoor dining in New York City in December even though his own tracing data showed that restaurants only accounted for 1.43 percent of the viral spread. It made no sense at all, but he shut it down anyway, throwing tens of thousands of people out of work just days before Christmas. Trust the science, in the end, wound up meaning little more than shut up and do what the government tells you to.

Chapter 6

Myth 5—The Great Leadership
of Andrew Cuomo

There was a period of time during early to mid-April in which New York Gov. Andrew Cuomo was arguably the most popular man in the United States. Serious writers at actual publications who get paid and everything were opining on the possibility that he could replace Joe Biden at the top of the Democratic ticket. The term Cuomosexual came into being for women, and presumably some men, so wowed by his governing prowess that they began thinking about him in, well, other ways.

This was a somewhat curious development seeing as New York had the highest case and death tolls in the country. By April 12, over ten thousand people had died of Covid in the Empire State, most in New York City. But generally speaking, the public, not just locally but nationally, seemed inclined to give Cuomo a pass because of the unique conditions in his state and its largest city. New York got hit early, it got hit hard, and the crush of humanity and shoulder-to-shoulder subway system had made it a deadly playground for the virus. It is also a hub of travel not just from China, but also from the European nations like Italy that also were hit hard early on. But what really captured the nation were Cuomo's tone and personality and the way in which it stood against the tone and personality of President Trump. Cuomo would hold a press conference every afternoon that became must-see TV for the stay-at-home lockdown set, otherwise known as almost everyone, and Trump would do his set with the task force in the early evening. The two shows offset each other, even when the information they contained was more or less the same, which frankly was quite a bit of the time.

It's not that Andrew Cuomo is the opposite of Donald Trump; he's not. Mike Pence is the opposite of Donald Trump. Pence is a staid, soft-spoken Midwestern guy with a twenty-dollar haircut who doesn't have lunch alone with women he's not married to. He's so boring most of the time that drying paint listens to him and says, "Jeez, is this guy done yet?" But sometimes, that is exactly what is needed. It was what always made Pence an effective vice president for Trump: no drama, dependable, and as predictable as a Harlem Globetrotters game. Andrew Cuomo is actually very similar to Donald Trump in a lot of ways. Both grew up in Queens, New York, both had wealthy, powerful fathers in whose footsteps they followed, both have that rich kid from the outer borough chip on the shoulder, the need to show they are tough, not pampered, and both enjoy going off the cuff when addressing issues, sometimes into strange rants or stories that seem out of place.

Cuomo's father, Mario Cuomo, the former governor of New York from the 1980s who was often spoken of himself as a potential presidential candidate, was one of the best retail politicians I ever saw. When I was thirteen, I volunteered for the Dukakis campaign in Philadelphia. One day, the elder Cuomo came to town to stump for Dukakis with Sens. Chris Dodd and Bill Bradley. When they went to South Philly, home of the Italian Market (and the Italian mob), the little old ladies couldn't have been more thrilled with Mario if Christ himself had showed up. He was a genuine hero to them.

Andrew Cuomo had never really exhibited that kind of star power until the pandemic and lockdown hit. Most of the corporate media, including his brother Chris at CNN, immediately set up Cuomo as the anti-Trump, or Bizarro Trump. Trump lies, they said, Cuomo tells the truth, Trump ignores science, they said, Cuomo trusts and respects his scientific advisors. It was like if Goofus and Gallant were goombahs from Queens and only one of them had some kind of moral compass.

By this time, Joe Biden was the presumptive nominee and was already down in the basement waiting out the pandemic; he would not really emerge for another four months, when the conventions came. The Democrats needed a leader, a face of their response. Nancy Pelosi was coming off a brutal defeat in an impeachment she never really wanted; Chuck Schumer is arguably a gifted politician behind the scenes but not a "face." That really left only a few potential choices; along with Cuomo was California governor Gavin Newsom and Michigan governor Gretchen Whitmer. Of the three, Cuomo had the "it" factor, and being on the East Coast also gave his pressers a time slot advantage.

As early as March 17, CNN's Chris Cillizza had this to say: "The two men have emerged as the two most prominent figures in the country's attempts to limit the spread of coronavirus, and—perhaps not surprisingly given their partisan affiliations and broader views on governance—have repeatedly clashed over who is doing the right thing and who is, well, not." The truth, as is often the way, was a bit more complicated. In fact, throughout the first month of the lockdown, Cuomo and Trump would often praise each other, as would Trump and Newsom. They actually worked very well together in a quite a few instances; though they disagreed about how many were required, Trump would provide Cuomo with the ventilators he needed. The Army Corps of Engineers constructed a hospital in the Jacob Javits center in Manhattan, no mean feat as anyone who has ever loaded a trade show into that place knows. And on March 30 the hospital ship *USNS Comfort* arrived in New York Harbor, its slow passage in front of Lady Liberty offering one of the iconic images of the pandemic, and one of very few that felt more like hope than doom.

Though Cuomo and Trump sniped at each other—they are from Queens, after all—it was really the news media that set up the dichotomy between the two men that eventually fueled all the Cuomo love on the Left. This is something we would see the media do with Trump and his scientific advisers as well. Any slight difference between something said by the president and something said by Dr. Fauci would get blown up into a story about Trump denying science, when in fact it was again a difference in tone, and both men insisted most of the time that they had a good, or at least functioning, working relationship.

On April 13, Fauci would say that the president had been taking his advice, adding, "The first and only time that I went in and said we should do mitigation strongly, the response was, 'Yes, we'll do it.'" When he was pressed if he was saying this voluntarily, the implication being that Trump was forcing him to saying it, Fauci took offense, saying "Everything I do is voluntary; please don't ever say that." Stories like the pandemic and lockdown need a hero and a villain, it was obvious who the villain would be to a corporate media fixated on destroying Donald Trump, but what they did not know was that their chosen hero, Andrew Cuomo, though perfectly cast, had made some decisions that would come back to haunt him and them.

I asked Ari Fleischer, former White House press secretary under George W. Bush about why this halo had been placed upon the head of the governor of New York State, and he rather confirmed my suspicions, stating, "The press fell in love with him because they saw him as the anti-Trump. Cuomo screamed bloody murder and blamed Trump and the federal government for New York's problems. The press loved it, because they routinely boost anti-Trump voices, regardless of whether the criticism has merit. If Trump is the villain, Cuomo is the antivillain, with the acquiescence of the press."

This hit the mark not just in regard to Cuomo, but in regard to almost every single bit of coverage of the virus and lockdown. The news always led with how Trump was wrong, or how he was misleading the country. It was part of the bigger media problem in the Trump presidency. Under Bush or Obama, when you watched an hour of cable news, either in the newsier daytime hours or the more pop-partisan evening, there was typically five or ten minutes about whatever the president was up to that day, and then the rest of the hour was dedicated to, you know, other news. During the Trump presidency, there simply was no other news; it was all Trump all the time and that is not a good way to keep a nation informed.

Also lacking coverage at almost every turn were the myriad times that Trump and Cuomo worked well together and complimented each other. Such incidents got about as much attention as a Volvo in a parking lot full of Lamborghinis. The concept of there being sides in the pandemic just kept getting worse, and if we are to be fair, it had far less to do with any substantive disagreements between Cuomo, or Newsom, or any Democrat and Trump; it had to do with the constant need for the media to pour fire on any small flagellation that popped up.

A careful look at Cuomo's actions and statements as the crisis was ramping up in March betrays how shambolic and disorganized his response really was. And it was very much his response having been granted the powers of a king by the state legislature. Stu Burguiere would eventually create a Twitter thread that put in stark perspective how confusing and contradictory Cuomo's reaction really was.

On March 12, for example, the governor would say, "There's not going to be any quarantine; individual mobility is what we're all about." The next day, he would tell MSNBC that he didn't think the crisis was "any different here than anywhere else. The anxiety and the fear are as much of a problem as the virus." That sounds an awful lot like President Trump saying that he didn't want to cause a panic and that the cure cannot be worse than the disease.

On March 17, the quietest Saint Patrick's Day in New York City history, Cuomo responded to New York City mayor Bill de Blasio suggesting a shelter-in-place order might be needed by saying there would be no shelter-in-place order. The next day, he reiterated this position, "…that is not going to happen, shelter in place, for New York City." The very next day, Cuomo would order offices to reduce their capacity, but still shrugged off quarantine. "Are we reducing density? Yes. Are we going to do quarantine, are people imprisoned in their homes? No."

On March 20, Cuomo would completely reverse course. By executive order, he began New York PAUSE. Everything he had promised would not happen happened. Cuomo might have been slow to lock down, but once he got there, he stayed there, and so did New York. The people in state and local government I interviewed believed, as Joe Borelli told me, this would last maybe thirty days, just until the hospitals were in order. Nobody had any idea at all that twelve months later, significant parts of the lockdown would still be in place.

Let's be honest: you have to wake up pretty early in the morning to make Bill de Blasio look like an effective leader, but that, at least in hindsight, is exactly was Andrew Cuomo managed to pull off. The effect on New York of all of Cuomo's vacillating was a confused whiplash. Although it is true that by mid-April, New York City had all the hospital space it needed, between about April 5 and April 18, the deaths in the state were mounting dramatically, averaging around one thousand a day. It was as bad as the crisis would get in New York, and it was very bad. To put this in perspective, Florida, which has a higher population than New York, was averaging under fifty deaths per day during this time, and even at the height of its death toll, the Sunshine State would still only see about 276 deaths in a single a day.

On April 3, I ran a piece at the *Federalist* titled "We Cannot Destroy the Country for the Sake of New York City." It would be the first time that I would experience serious negative backlash to a piece arguing against mass lockdowns; it would not be the last. What was becoming apparent, and why I wrote the piece, was that New York, in particular New York City, faced unique challenges that made it much more susceptible to fast spread. This included general population density, a vast public transit system, as well as the challenge of communicating Coronavirus information to a population that speaks over two hundred languages. To me and to a growing number of others, it did not make sense to apply a one-size-fits-all approach to the virus when conditions on the ground varied so dramatically from place to place. Part of the disconnect here was the adoration of Cuomo. If, as the media insisted, his was the responsible approach to the virus, then surely that was true not only in New York, but for all of America. But as I wrote in the piece, New York, notwithstanding the general opinion of New Yorkers, is not the universe.

I had occasion this week, as the virus ground us all to a stop, to talk to a friend in Indiana. I asked, "Is this the greatest crisis the country has ever faced?" We haven't been invaded since 1812, I pointed out, and have never been occupied. Her reply, "What crisis?" She was in her backyard, her children playing. My life was at a bizarre standstill, death all around; hers was not. Yet all across the nation I don't have time to think about, lives are being destroyed not by the virus, but by an economic disaster unknown in a century.

The entire country, experts I trust tell us, must be shut down. Businesses shuttered, many with little hope of opening again. Ten million people unemployed in two weeks. Ten million. In that world beyond that Hudson River, an economic hammer is falling faster than the virus can spread. *Who can think of money at a time like this?* we are told. *How callous.* But it's not just money. In its own way, it's lives; it is a way of life.

Jack Kerouac—who danced and played and was educated in New York City but found his literary and intellectual fortune in the forgotten America—once said he didn't want a living; he wanted a life. But where is the difference? What is life if not the ability to sustain it? We are embarking on the devastation of an entire nation when it is becoming clearer and clearer that the gravest threat lies in megacities. And no city is more mega than Gotham.

Max Diamond, writing at the *Washington Post* in response to my piece, as well as others by Manhattan Institute's Heather MacDonald and Prager U's Dennis Prager, wrote, "Perhaps the most reliable worry of conservative media is that, as the president tweeted last month, "WE CANNOT LET THE CURE BE WORSE THAN THE PROBLEM ITSELF." Writing for the *Federalist*, in an article headlined, "We Cannot Destroy the Country for the Sake of New York City," David Marcus said, "We need to make some hard choices."[32] But instead of spelling out what those choices are or evaluating economic expertise against the advice of public health experts, he cited Beat author Jack Kerouac for advice on Coronavirus policy: per Marcus, Kerouac once said that "he didn't want a living, he wanted a life." Marcus responds: "But where is the difference? What is life if not the ability to sustain it?" The suggestion being, apparently, that it is acceptable to sacrifice the vulnerable for the sake of our standard of living.

Clearly, every day that the country is in lockdown mode, working people risk losing incomes, health coverage, and savings. But the reason we're staying at home is that, according to the experts, not the commentariat, the virus's spread is worse than the alternative..."

Though I obviously disagreed with Diamond, who identifies as a conservative and had written for the *Federalist*, though I didn't know him, there was something positive about the piece. There was finally recognition that the lockdown was indeed harmful, and not just to the stock market. After well over a month of complaints from the Left that conservatives and Trump were more worried about stock portfolios, or some vague notion of "the economy" than they were in saving lives, the recognition that lockdowns were taking a harsh toll not only on average people's pocketbooks, but on their mental and physical health began to emerge.

Although in April the presidential election was still only in the back of people's Covid-addled minds, and we were months away from the start of genuine campaign season, the question of federal versus local response to the virus was already forming as a central issue. Critics of the president and the administration's approach chided Trump for not having a "national plan." This criticism would grow throughout the summer and into the fall.

For his part, Trump was clear very early on that he intended to take a federalist approach, in which Washington provided resources for the states, but the governors decided for each of their states how those resources should be used and to what extent they would lock down their economies. Nobody was ever clear about what that national plan should have been; presumably, it really did mean grafting Cuomo's severe New York approach to the entire nation. How this could have even been done is not clear, as evidenced by Joe Biden's inability to present a clear alternative that he would embrace beyond showing better leadership and setting a better example.

But stories began to bubble up that would transform by-then Emperor Cuomo's halo into a crown of thorns. Under the governor's direction, elderly patients infected with Covid were being sent into nursing homes where they were infecting other residents; more than anything else, that decision led to the mounting death tolls in April. For all the talk of Trump's mismanagement of the virus, if there was a smoking gun pointing to poor leadership during the pandemic, it was this decision by Cuomo. To add insult to this injury, or frankly death, Cuomo insisted that no investigation into this terrible decision was required. With very few exceptions, the media was complicit in this lack of curiosity into their hero's grave mistake. Narrative, after all, comes first.

As it turned out, Cuomo did not succeed in staving off investigation. By February, New York Attorney General Letitia James would release a bruising report showing that Cuomo's administration had undercounted nursing home deaths by up to 50 percent, representing as many as ten thousand lives. Soon after, one of his aides admitted that they had slow-walked the Department of Justice on the numbers because they feared the DOJ investigation was politically motivated. The water was growing hotter and then suddenly boiled over.

By March, two women who worked for Cuomo would accuse him of sexual harassment. Finally, the corporate media was ready to throw him under the bus. That says a lot about the media's priorities. When Cuomo made decisions leading to the deaths of ten thousand people, it was a minor story, but the sexual harassment cases blew up. After all, the latter did not implicate the media fawning from months before. But in an almost Shakespearean way, and lightning fast, Cuomo was thrown unceremoniously under the bus. Out in California, Gavin Newsom wasn't doing much better; he faced a serious recall challenge. In short, the supposedly great leaders of the pandemic's early days fell from very great heights. So far, in fact, did they fall that further political careers for both would seem very much in doubt.

Chapter 7

Myth 6—The Lockdowns Aren't So Bad

T. S. Elliot famously wrote that April is cruelest month. 2020 certainly had his back on that as it ushered in its own silent wasteland of empty streets and frustrated people locked in their abodes. As the calendar turned to an April Fools' Day less funny than any in recent memory. I had been basically stuck in my apartment for almost three weeks, my only sojourns into my Brooklyn nabe to the bodega, grocery store, liquor store, and visits with my weed guy. At some point, I realized that the latter was the only person I had actually had physical contact with, as we never stopped shaking hands upon greeting each other.

For many people, including me, the lockdown meant a whole lot time in your own head, and I spent much of it in my backyard as the days grew longer and warmer, smoking cigarettes and drinking Jameson in my *Federalist* tumbler. I was writing more than I ever had, even before starting this book in the summer, but that still filled up only so much of the day. Much time was spent in silent meditation, not unlike my childhood experiences in Quaker prep school enduring Meeting for Worship once a week.

One specific irony that I was dealing with was that at the start of the new year, I had dedicated myself to being more social and going out more. OK, now that you have stopped laughing, I can say that the reason for this was that in the seven months or so since Libby had moved out, I had been a bit of a hermit. I had almost always found ways to get out of social events or gatherings, and spent almost all my time when Charlie wasn't with me, so about half of every week, basically by myself. Now, even Charlie was gone.

Libby and I had moved in together when we were twenty, married at twenty-three, which, in our social circles, was even stranger than having done it at a big Catholic church. The upshot was that neither of us had ever lived on our own as adults. I'll be honest and admit it was something I didn't even know I could do, and that scared me a little. The split itself could not have been more amicable; I say split because as of writing this, we still aren't actually divorced. I never even hired a lawyer.

In late 2019, I did get served the papers; Libby had given me a heads-up that they were coming. I remember being on my front porch, seeing the guy climb sheepishly out of his car with a binder. I knew it was him. My first thought was to wonder if this was a tipping situation. I figured it couldn't be an easy job, so I slipped him a ten spot, glanced at the papers, and shoved them in a drawer.

Without getting into too much detail, as this is not ultimately a book about my shortcomings, our split owed almost exclusively to my drinking, which had always been copious but had come to usher in more mean-spiritedness and less control of my emotional state. I ignored what I can now see were firm warnings from Libby and thus found myself by myself.

In the first few weeks, the lockdown did not help my situation with alcohol; in fact, and I think this is true for many Americans, it just kind of made it worse. A lot of my friends, maybe even most of them, were joking about all the day drinking they were doing, but like any good joke, there was some sad truth beneath it. In August, the *Lancet* would release a study that found, "In summary, lockdown represents a risk factor for increasing alcohol consumption in people with alcohol use disorders and relapse for those who were previously abstinent. Those who do relapse are at a high risk of harmful drinking and require a tailored approach for follow-up and intervention. Support from alcohol liaison services could prevent relapse during lockdown."

It all made a kind of perfect sense, of course. The cocktail, so to speak, of being stuck in the house with nowhere to go, the sense of foreboding and dread hovering about society, the fact that liquor stores were among the only ones open, and drinking in general moving from a social situation in a bar to a lonely situation in one's living room all fed the desire of Americans to find escape and solace at the bottom of a bottle.

For me, things began to change in regard to all of this on April 6.

It was a Monday, so I dialed into the weekly *Federalist* staff meeting at 10 a.m. with a hangover that would have made Charles Bukowski say, "Dude." I was shaky, only vaguely following the threads of conversation. I had about a shot in the bottle from the night before so I downed it. The shaking subsided, but my mind wasn't there, and at some point, probably when the conversation turned to our coverage of reality TV, I kind of just decided that something seriously had to change. I decided that I would stop drinking hard alcohol, at least at home, something I had done, with extremely rare exceptions, every day for at least the past fifteen years.

For whatever reason, it seemed to stick. This was a pledge I had made in the past, which had always failed. But this was different. In the past, those attempts had more to do with what other people, mainly Libby, thought of me; it was something I was doing for the sake of others, but here, as Shakespeare put it, was not a creature but myself. This time, I was doing it for me. And incredibly, it lasted a week, then another, and so on until now, in December, with the exception of parties (to the extent they existed) and dinners out where I would have a cocktail or two, it stuck.

It worked for most of 2020. But by March of 2021 after a few months of dark, cold lockdown in Gotham, a very different and more brutal version than the Spring variety, I spun out into a bad spiral. Twelve months after the whole thing started, I found myself at the airport on my way to rehab in California. But that is a story for another day.

The next Sunday would be Easter. I wrote about what a strange day it would be for the *Post*, and since it was edited by Sohrab Ahmari, arguably the leading Catholic conservative thinker of his generation, I didn't have to hold back on the God stuff. It's actually interesting; when I was writing more widely, for places like *National Review*, and the *Weekly Standard*, the *New York Times*, and similar publications, I always felt that in my writing, I had to refer to my Catholic faith but not profess it. At the *Federalist* and in Ahmari's opinion change, that was not the case. I did not have to write that some believe Jesus was the Son of God; I could just straight-up call Jesus the Son of God. It may seem like a small difference, but in fact, it is not. It is a pointed attempt to bring faith back into a more central place in American life.

Among the cruel ironies of the Coronavirus lockdown was the fact that the lockdown itself prohibited Americans from most of the very events and rituals in which they find their peace. This included weddings, family reunions, concerts, and plays. But perhaps most fundamental for millions or believers was the inability to attend church in person. The ban on church attendance was also one of the most constitutionally fraught issues of the response; after all, the founding document could scarcely be clearer on our right to attend church.

As a Catholic, this was a very difficult thing for me. Although the cardinals and bishops gave dispensation for not attending Mass, the inability to receive the sacraments, especially the Eucharist, was something I felt deeply. In the senior circuit of Christianity, partaking of the body of Christ is not a metaphor; it is a literal moment of becoming one with God, accepting Him and knowing that though you are not worthy, He has accepted you.

I had spent the last day of 2019 in Baltimore on a moving job with my buddy Brad. We liked to do longer hauls together, load up a truck in New York City in the morning, then spend a day driving, find a hotel, and go hop some bars. It just so happened that on December 31, I awoke, oddly refreshed after a night out with Brad, at a hotel just steps from the cathedral in Baltimore. It's a marvelous building designed by the one of the architects of the U.S. Capitol building. I expected Mass to be in the light and airy upstairs church, but instead found myself and a few others praying at year's twilight in the dark catacombs below. I prayed for blessings in the coming year.

By the time the edict came down barring church attendance in March, I had been doing a pretty decent job of getting to church, going to confession, and doing all the right religious things in 2020. I was also making an effort to get out more, enjoy people, escape the cave of my apartment that I entered like a bear hibernating for the first near year as an adult that I had ever lived alone—well, not alone; I still had Charlie two or three nights a week and for part of most days, but without Libby.

That first Sunday of shuttered churches, I recall sitting in my backyard and hearing the church bells from St. Ephraim's. I crossed myself and prayed to the Blessed Mother, always to the Blessed Mother, and wondered at the ancient peel of the bells, a sound as familiar in the Middle Ages as in the Brooklyn of modern realities—just like plagues, it would seem. I thought of all the people finding their new ways to be with God in isolation.

When I began working at the *Federalist*, one of the things that kind of amazed me was how open the staff was about religion. I guess this makes sense since it is a journal of politics, religion, and culture, but it was a very new experience for me. In my two decades in theater, religion, and especially Christianity, was generally either ignored or insulted. I knew one or two other practicing Catholics in the New York theater scene, but it was mostly something to keep quiet about.

The first time I saw a prayer request on a *Federalist* email list, I was therefore somewhat shocked. Suddenly, my faith in God was not something to hide but something to be shared, even in the workplace. This is not to say that everyone was Christian or religious by any means; I often remember David Harsanyi, an atheist of Jewish descent now at *National Review*, chiming in on those threads with his nonreligious best wishes for whatever the problem being prayed over was.

I mention this because the corporate media for the most part, indeed the corporate world, operates much more like theater in terms of religion than the *Federalist* does. It's almost like the way people used to look at homosexuality: "I don't care what you do in your bedroom, but keep it to yourself." Just replace church for bedroom. This became a massive media blind spot throughout the shutdown. So far removed were so many producing the news from the regular practice of religion that they utterly failed to understand just what an imposition the ban against church truly was. Suddenly, atheists and nonpracticing Christians were all theologists who attested to the fact that the building doesn't matter, the gathering doesn't matter, God is in your heart: "My God" they would say, "would rather you protect the vulnerable than worship Him at Church." Everyone became an amateur Aquinas as if nobody had ever thought about any of this over the past two thousand years.

For many Americans, church still is the center of their community life, and while early on, for the first few weeks, even the most religious of folks understood the need to close them down, as time wore on, questions began to mount. Are liquor stores and even strip clubs really essential and church is not? Why were even socially distant services such as attempts at drive-in church being shut down as well? It began to feel like it was less about science, or the actual path of the virus, and more about cementing the social contract we had all apparently made to isolate ourselves.

It certainly felt like no accident that Ash Wednesday was on February 26, just days before the lockdowns would take hold. That made the first several weeks of stay-at-home feel very much like Christ's forty days in the desert that the Lenten season commemorates. Without Mass, with only the church bells and my bible, I felt in a new way the temptations of the

Lord as I imagine many other Christians did. Lent became uniquely personal and meaningful.

To no small extent, America can be divided between those who attend church and those who do not. Somewhere between 35 and 40 percent of Americans attend church on a weekly basis in the United States. But one would never know this from our popular entertainment and news media. In fact, one of the things that has always made the TV show *The Simpsons* stand out is that they go to church. So it is little surprise that our corporate media elite would look at religion as a luxury, not something essential to our lives.

I naively thought we were getting toward to the end of this. We were two weeks past the two weeks to flatten the curve, after all. When Easter came, there was no church, of course, no place really to go, so I met up with friend Natasha Simons, an editor for Simon and Schuster, at the Greenwood cemetery in Brooklyn, oddly one of the 19th century's most famous parks and picnic destinations. My first subway ride in nearly a month was eerie and empty, but just a few stops, and the day was lovely; as it turned out, Bill de Blasio was there at the same time, though we didn't know that until later. We wandered the monuments to the long dead and when I got home, I FaceTimed Charlie and tried to help him set up the *Fortnite* V-Bucks gift card in the basket of goodies I had sent him.

It was not long after Easter that something began happening, bubbling up first in the Midwest and then spreading across various parts of the country. They were antilockdown protests. Among the first to gain widespread media attention was a protest in Michigan organized by the Michigan Conservative Coalition, along with other groups. Thousands of cars drove en masse to the state capitol, with hundreds gathered outside of it. These people were angry and ready to get back to their lives and jobs. At a time when news media outlets, especially those on the Right, were just beginning to gently question the efficacy of the lockdowns, some the people of Michigan, to the frustration of the governor, Gretchen Whitmer, were ahead of that curve.

This interview in a report from the *Detroit Free Press* stood out. "Justin Heyboer of Alto, an owner of Wildwood Family Farms, said his family has been in business for four generations and the order is financially crippling on several fronts. The company does landscaping, has greenhouses, hosts weddings and has a liquor license, he said. "This is our busiest time of year," said Heyboer, who drove to Lansing for the demonstration dubbed "Operation Gridlock" because organizers said they wanted to gain attention by tying up traffic.

"I'd rather die from the Coronavirus than see a generational company be gone."

Heyboer later said he feels "very strongly about the stay-home order but wished he had chosen different words to express that."

There is a lot to unpack here. Mostly around the statement that the gentleman made and then came to regret. For the better part of a month, the entire country had been focused almost entirely on avoiding deaths. Here was someone speaking of something as relatively meaningless as a business being more important. I can understand why he walked it back, but I can also understand where it came from. Losing a generational family business, or farm, or property may not be as bad as dying, but it is far from nothing, and for politicians and the media to be so dismissive of it was flat-out infuriating. I could readily understand why people like him were frustrated, if not outraged, by politicians and journalists who were still cashing their paychecks lecturing them about what is really important in life. Those on the losing end of the lockdown were basically being told to sit down and shut up.

Among the protestors, Trump hats and paraphernalia were plentiful; this would kick off a balancing act by president Trump, who clearly had sympathy for the protests but was also attempting to create as little distance as possible between his own statements and those of his medical experts. But the right-wing media was far less shy in assessing the protests, much to the chagrin of progressive media outlets like *Columbia*

Journalism Review, which reported on conservative media reaction this way.

"Whatever the source of the antilockdown protests, right-wing media has thrown its weight behind them.[33] Talk radio hosts, Twitter pundits such as Candace Owens, and sites including *Infowars* and the *Gateway Pundit* have all played their part, as have stars of Fox News. On Wednesday, Tucker Carlson called Whitmer's shutdown policies "mindless and authoritarian" and accused her of careerism.[34] (She's been widely touted, of late, as a possible vice-presidential pick for Joe Biden.) Jeanine Pirro said, of the protesters, 'God bless them.' Laura Ingraham, addressing them on Twitter, wrote that it's 'time to get your freedom back.' Yesterday, Brian Kilmeade, a host on *Fox & Friends*, said that lockdown orders were 'getting ridiculous.'[35] Harris Faulkner, another Fox host, asked Mike Huckabee, the former Arkansas governor and right-wing pundit, 'This country was kind of founded on people who were willing to risk themselves for freedom: Is that what this is, or something else?' Huckabee said it was not something else."[36]

However one felt about the protests, and obviously opinion differed greatly, particularly along political lines, it did set in place some basic tenets that would animate the antilockdown arguments from others, myself included, that would continue to grow into May and June. On a very important level, it was a matter of constitutional rights. This wasn't something people paid a lot of attention to in the early days of the lockdown. Emergency powers are something that Americans had been through before. But at the same time, we have a Bill of Rights, not a Bill of Rights Unless There Is an Emergency.

As the lockdown entered its second month, we as a nation were also entering unprecedented territory in terms of the length and scope of emergency powers. Certainly, during World War II, we had limitations like price controls set by the Office of Price Administration, which was set up by executive order, but just two months into America's involvement in the war, Congress passed the Emergency Price Control Act, which placed limitations on the agency. This is the balance that the Constitution requires, a balance that would be ignored for months on end in states across America.

So off went the parade of cars and trucks, many emblazoned with signs for President Trump. There was the odd Confederate battle flag, which of course the media and progressives seized on as evidence that these were just a bunch of toothless, racist yokels. And there were guns. Lots of guns. And the guns played differently depending where in America one lives. For someone like me, in New York City, the idea of hundreds of armed protestors is bizarre and a little scary. My personal opinion on guns is that everyone should have the right to own them, but I choose not to. Mostly because I'm worried I would forget where I put it or something; I'm just not that responsible and it's good to know one's limitations. So I well understood why so many Americans were freaked out by what they saw.

But at the same time, there really was no violence, either in Michigan or in the myriad copycat protests that grew across the Midwest and South. To the extent that there were counterprotestors, they were also nonviolent, and so what the protests amounted to was much more a spectacle than a crisis. This, of course, did not stop the media from hyperventilating about what was coming to be known as "superspreader events."

Chapter 8

⸺◇⸺

Myth 7—Southern Governors Engaged in Human Sacrifice

In the second half of April, the federalist approach taken by the Trump administration, which left decisions regarding the lockdowns very much up to individual states, began to result in divergent courses in different regions. Two governors in particular would come to personify the desire to open the economy; those were Ron DeSantis of Florida and Brian Kemp of Georgia.

These governors both made the decision to begin reopening in late April to the wailing and gnashing of teeth of much of the corporate media. The *Atlantic* would hysterically call Kemp's reopening plan an "experiment in human sacrifice." CNN's Dr. Sanjay Gupta, the crown prince of Covid panic, warned that Kemp was falling into a trap; he suggested that within two weeks of reopening, Georgia would see a spike in cases and deaths. Another phrase of the pandemic would come into being: "Just wait two weeks." Over the next few months, every time a state opened up, or some large-scale event would occur and the virus numbers didn't surge, we would be told to "Just wait two weeks." But just as happened with the initial two weeks to flatten the curve, every time a holocaust of Coronavirus didn't come to pass, we were told to just wait another fortnight.

On Tuesday, April 21 at the White House Task Force briefing, even Donald Trump would throw Gov. Kemp under the bus. "I told the governor of Georgia, Brian Kemp, that I disagree strongly with his decision to open certain facilities which are in violation of the phase one guidelines for the incredible people of Georgia," he said. This came as a bit of a surprise, as reporting had suggested that Trump supported the efforts to get back to some degree of normalcy. Trump went so far as to say that if he saw "something egregious" in Georgia, he would step in. It's not clear what exactly he meant by stepping in. For all the talk, especially from Democrats, about the need for a national plan, it was never clear what if any authority the president had to compel states to follow the federal guidelines.

Trump was rhetorically hedging his bet, but his overall game plan was the same. Provide material support for states and guidelines from the task force, but then allow those states to make their own decisions. And even though he disavowed Kemp's plan to allow some businesses to open, it was hard not to get the sense that he was at least somewhat sympathetic to the idea, especially since in mid-April, in response to the antilockdown protests, Trump had tweeted, "Liberate Michigan." Just as in January and February, the president was trying to take a balanced approach, but that is not his forte; in fact, he is awful at it, and the media and his political opponents were eager to point out the mixed nature of his message.

But Kemp and DeSantis had other ideas. This should have been an occasion for reasonable and measured disagreement, not only that, but an opportunity to compare the results of total shutdown, at least the American version of it, and partial reopening. Of course Kemp and DeSantis knew that they were taking a risk; of course more cases would result from their decision. The question was whether a spike could be avoided so the uptick could be managed. There were certainly those who argued that any increase had to be avoided, but increasingly the economic and human toll of keeping everyone shuttered was a powerful counterbalance. The two weeks after Florida and Georgia went rogue, not to mention the months after, show that these states took a reasonable, if not the certifiably best, approach. These states never experienced the spikes feared by the naysayers, and what is more, they did far better economically as people got back to work.

On April 20, Georgia had eighty-five Covid deaths; that number would stay relatively steady aside from a flash spike in early November that quickly subsided. Florida saw no large increase in deaths until late July, but at no point were the hospital resources in danger of being overwhelmed, and there was nothing even remotely close to the spike in deaths we saw in New York City, where on March 22, there were forty-seven deaths, and on April 7, there were over a thousand. Put simply, the experiment in human sacrifice did not come to pass. We waited two weeks, then another, then another, and a devastating spike in lives lost just never occurred, notwithstanding people getting haircuts and eating in restaurants.

By September, New York State would have an unemployment rate of 9.75 percent; by contrast, Florida had an unemployment rate of 7.6 percent. By August, the *New York Times* was reporting that one-third of all small businesses in New York City could be gone forever. By December, one in eight chain stores; many of them franchises, were closed for good. In fairness, New York did keep its case numbers and deaths lower than Florida throughout the summer, though by that time, the virus had already ravaged vulnerable populations like the elderly residents of old folks homes that Cuomo sent infected patients into. But to go back to the original theory of the case, Florida and Georgia did have relatively flat curves.

Throughout May, as the "experiment" in the South proved at the very least not to be a disaster, the news media utterly failed to balance the two now-distinct approaches to the virus and compare them in a rational way. And we should call this what it is: rank, partisan dishonesty. Instead, Cuomo and DeSantis, much like Cuomo and Trump had been, were thrust into a kind of battle between good and evil. Cuomo was good and DeSantis was bad; it was as simple as that. Did the science matter? Did the numbers matter? Each week that went by, the Democrats and the media seemed more disconnected from reality, less willing to admit previous mistakes. It was if they had never told us not to touch our faces, or to wear gloves, or to wipe down our groceries; all, they had assured us, were vital measures, and all had turned out to be next to useless.

In mid-April I got a call from my friend Ryan Williams, who was in Palm Beach. Ryan is always somewhere like Palm Beach, or the Cape, or Geneva. He's a former Romney comms guy who is now in PR. I first met him on a whirlwind junket for Philip Morris where he took Billy McMorris of the *Washington Free Beacon* and me to Switzerland and Poland. Billy convinced me to go with Mass with him in Warsaw and I recall us both being excited to go to confession with a Polish-speaking priest—we could really let loose—but it turned out the guy spoke English.

Ryan had a mini scoop for me about a consulting firm working with Cuomo on contact tracing and a reopening plan. But before we got to that, I wanted to know how things were in Florida. As I stood smoking in my chilly backyard, still basically on a stay-at-home order, Ryan made me marvel at tales of dinners indoors and happy people wandering around maskless. It was obvious that he was in a very different place than I was. America was heading into a summer in which no states or even cities would have quite the same rules and regulations, in which the supposedly shared experience of the lockdown varied widely, and often invisibly, as accounts from more open communities were far less common than tales of shutdowns on the coasts.

The story he was pitching me had to do with the McKinsey consulting firm. This time, he wasn't really promoting one of his clients, but more throwing shade at a rival. But just because people have agendas doesn't mean they aren't telling the truth: you just have to take the agenda into account and double-check. The crux of the story was that McKinsey had been tapped by Cuomo to create a Trump-proof reopening plan for New York. What raised the red flag, so to speak, was McKinsey's incredibly close ties to Communist China and its willingness to gloss over the human rights abuses there.

On April 23, Tucker Carlson would have McKinsey senior partner Peter Walker on his show to discuss the company's ties to the Communist regime. Maybe Ryan had called Tucker too. In the interview, Walker offered praise for the radical response of China to the pandemic, a response that literally saw people locked in their domiciles and snatched off the street. This was the company that Cuomo had turned to in order to create a plan that would counter that of the supposedly fascist Donald Trump.

Cuomo had created a coalition of seven East Coast states; it was New Jersey's Gov. Murphy who would say their goal was to create a plan that was "Trump proof." Why it had to be Trump proof proved to be a bit of a mystery. At the time, the president supported a staggered approach in which states at lower risk would start opening as was happening in Florida and Georgia, having backed off his criticism of Gov. Kemp. No effort was being made to strong-arm northeastern states into abandoning their lockdowns beyond the occasional presidential tweets about "liberation." The selection of China and shutdown-friendly McKinsey to help create the response plan only reinforced the idea that Cuomo had no interest in observing how other states were handling the crisis and adjusting based on what he saw. Rather, his was a my-way-or-the-highway approach that was increasingly little more than a constant rebuking of Trump.

The fact that Cuomo would bring in McKinsey to help him consolidate his power and to help him keep his state's citizens locked down should have raised grave concerns. Who were these powerful corporate consultants beholden to? It sure as hell was not the American people. These were apologists for the CCP. They had absolutely no business being involved in decisions that would suspend the rights of New Yorkers. It was as if our state legislature had been replaced by a Chinese lap dog in a fancy suit. It was no great surprise months later, after Biden won the election, that he would choose Obama administration alumna Louisa Terrell to head his office of legislative affairs. What had she been doing while Trump was in office? She was the head of public affairs for, you guessed it, McKinsey. It is well worth asking just how much power these unelected globalists really have.

By May 23, about a month into Gov. Kemp's decision to open parts of his economy, the *LA Times* would run a piece titled, "Georgia Opened First: What the Data Show Is A Matter of Fierce Debate." The headline was abject nonsense. The article admits the following, "When Georgia began to allow hair and nail salons, gyms and tattoo parlors to open their doors, some critics predicted that cases, hospitalizations and deaths would surge. That has not happened, but public health experts said it is still too early to measure the effect of reopening." In other words, "just wait two more weeks." But the spike never materialized.

So what was the other side of this supposedly fierce debate? It was that Georgia was using a combination of testing current cases and using antibody tests to discover past cases and using that as its denominator to determine the percentage of positive tests. But this choice was obviously irrelevant to the outcomes in hospitalizations and deaths that had been the result of Kemp's policy. This was a part of an insidious pattern: no matter what, when it turned out that Trump or any Republican had been right, the media would simply refuse to admit it. The president never got credit for correctly stating the infection fatality rate in March, and DeSantis and Kemp never got credit for striking a solid balance between medical and economic concerns in April and May.

The most galling thing about the myth that DeSantis and Kemp, among others like South Dakota's Kristie Noem, had acted recklessly and without care for the safety of their citizens is that when the prophesies of doom failed to come to pass, there was absolutely no reckoning in the media. They had gotten it badly wrong, but they didn't see it that way. This is because in their own minds they could never be wrong so long as they were in opposition to Trump and following the advice of the selected scientists.

By this time, Dr. Fauci had become one of the most famous and trusted men in America. Fauci worked very hard on behalf of the American people and deserves credit and thanks for that. But he also got some significant things wrong, like the China travel ban and the flip-flop on masking. That's not a knock on Fauci; that's how science works, but it made the cult the media created around him strange and suspicious. After the vaccine trials were successful and three former presidents committed to taking the vaccine, President-Elect Biden would say that he would take it if Dr. Fauci said it was OK. Why? As Pete Rose once said of Nolan Ryan, "Nolan Ryan's Nolan Ryan, but he's not God." Why would Fauci's OK mean more than the FDA's, the actual agency tasked with approving a vaccine? It was kabuki theater, another example of the American people not being given facts, but rather being told to rely on the fatherly expertise of flawed individuals

Chapter 9

⎯⎯◆⎯⎯

Myth 8—Extended Lockdowns Work

In 1969, the seminal moment of the Baby Boomer generation took place as thousands of young people descended on Woodstock, New York, to attend a music festival while rolling around in filthy muck, not taking showers, and engaging in free love. But there is a part of the Woodstock story that always gets left out. It took place during one of the worst flu pandemics of the 20th century. In fact, that strain of flu, known as the Hong Kong flu, which appeared a year earlier, apparently without controversy, killed one hundred thousand Americans at a time when the population numbered two hundred million. Until the Covid crisis, many, even most Americans had no idea that this pandemic ever happened. It didn't crush the American or global economy; there were no lockdowns or stay-at-home orders.

This is not the Middle Ages and the Black Death we are talking about here. it was merely fifty years ago. These are the people who put a man on the moon. Though science has advanced, the basic understanding of how viruses work remains similar if not unchanged. What was a blip on the cultural landscape then will be the defining moment of a generation now, but how effective was the lockdown? Did it work? Can it be the model we use going forward?

In September of 2020, a document came out called the Great Barrington Declaration. It was a most devastating attack on the efficacy of lockdowns, one that not only called into question the efficacy of the approach, but also denounced the brutal unintended consequences, especially among the poor, that lockdowns create. No punches were pulled as the authors wrote that:

"Coming from both the left and right, and around the world, we have devoted our careers to protecting people. Current lockdown policies are producing devastating effects on short and long-term public health. The results (to name a few) include lower childhood vaccination rates, worsening cardiovascular disease outcomes, fewer cancer screenings and deteriorating mental health—leading to greater excess mortality in years to come, with the working class and younger members of society carrying the heaviest burden. Keeping students out of school is a grave injustice.

"Keeping these measures in place until a vaccine is available will cause irreparable damage, with the underprivileged disproportionately harmed."

A few weeks later, it was the World Health Organization coming out to warn against extended lockdowns. Dr. David Nabarro, its special envoy for Covid-19, put it this way, "The only time we believe a lockdown is justified is to buy you time to reorganize, regroup, rebalance your resources, protect your health workers who are exhausted, but by and large, we'd rather not do it." That sounds a lot like two weeks to flatten the curve. Nabarro also pointed out the rather obvious fact that it is the global poor who suffer most under extended lockdowns.

There are two basic questions to ask regarding the effectiveness and wisdom of widespread lockdowns to combat the virus. First, how many lives did they save compared to not locking down, and second, did the costs of the lockdown outweigh the benefit? On both of these, the pro-lockdown position, which was the ubiquitous position of Democrats and most in the media, doesn't come off looking very good. In fact, the more we learn, the more that extended lockdowns look like a disastrous mistake.

The flashpoint for the debate over how many lives lockdowns save was, of all places, Sweden. Previously best known for bikini models and synthesized pop music, Sweden would chart a different course than most of the West when it came to Covid response measures, and in so doing, become the closest thing we have to a control group in the great experiment of 2020.

When looking at the case of Sweden, we face an enormous number of complicating factors. On the one hand, their open approach produced far more cases than we saw in its closest Scandinavian neighbors like Denmark and Finland, while the Swedes suffered 637 deaths per million people, Denmark would see 137 per million, Finland, seventy per million, and Norway, fifty-nine per million. On the other hand, when Sweden is compared to other Western nations such as the United States, the United Kingdom, and Spain, their numbers look much better.

When considering all this, we should remember the old baseball rule that in a close play, the tie goes to the runner. In this case, the tie must go to Sweden; this is because the Scandinavian nation managed to mitigate not only the economic downturn by keeping their businesses mostly open, but also other medical threats of locking down, including threats involving mental health, addiction, and people not seeking normal medical care, testing, and procedures. The question isn't simply which response method results in the fewest cases and deaths, but also how harmful to the society as a whole the approach is.

This was a point made by English writer Toby Young as his country and ours were on the verge of new lockdowns in November. In the *Critic*, he wrote,

"Lockdowns cause more loss of life than they prevent. This is contested, obviously, because the number of lives they've saved depends on a counterfactual generated by shonky computer models, and, on the other side of the equation, we don't yet know how much loss of life has been caused by the lockdowns. (For instance, unnecessary cancer deaths will occur over the next five years.) But given that the average age of the people whose lives are supposedly being saved is above 80, and given the tens of thousands of people who will die unnecessarily as a result of cancer screening programmes being postponed, cancer care being delayed, strokes and cardiovascular disease being untreated, elective surgeries being postponed, out-patient care being cancelled and the long-term impact of job losses on mortality, it seems overwhelmingly likely that lockdowns cause a net loss of life."

We saw this grim reality in the case of Sherwin Hall from Leeds, England. Hall had been begging for an MRI. It was only after thirteen visits to Leeds Teaching Hospital between March and the end of May that he was able to receive an MRI that showed tumors in his lungs. Had this been caught sooner, he may well have survived. And this was not an isolated incident; cancer screening in both the UK and America were down by as much as 90 percent during the height of the lockdowns. We will probably never know how many lives this cost.

One of the earliest critics of lockdowns in the United States and greatest champions of the Swedish approach would be Alex Berenson, a former *New York Times* reporter with a contrarian streak who was speaking out against extreme restrictions when most of us were not comfortable doing so yet. He would write two books during the pandemic exploring the relative effectiveness of shutdown measures. These positions put a target on Berenson's back, but for all the disdain thrown at him, one thing that did not ever happen was a serious challenge to his facts. Nothing he wrote or said had to be walked back or corrected. The plain fact of the matter, surprising though it may be, is that Berenson had a better batting average than Dr. Fauci, who on several occasions, including regarding masks and the China travel ban, had to walk back his statements.

But we don't have to go quite as far as Sweden to see an economy that chose to stay more open than most in the United States. Although no city was spared suffering and economic damage during the lockdown, cities that are heavily based on tourism and entertainment were doubly kneecapped. This certainly hurt places like New York City and Los Angeles, but perhaps no city in America relies so heavily on this sector of the economy as Las Vegas. In fact, it is more or less the only reason Las Vegas ever came into being. The brainchild of gangster Meyer Lansky, Sin City was founded as a gambling mecca when wagering was illegal in most places and as the place the biggest stars of stage, screen, and radio plied their trade in the smoky clubs of Nevada wonder.

So it really should not come as a surprise that the city and its mayor Carolyn Goodman were anxious to get things back to something like normal as fast as possible. After all, this is not work people can do from home: this is housekeeping and bartending and blackjack dealing and live performing. And it wasn't just the lockdown and stay-at-home orders locally; it was the fact that few people felt comfortable getting on a plane to the extent that they were even flights. The oasis of fun in the desert was drying up, and it was drying up fast.

I visited Las Vegas in early September; almost six months after its lockdown began. It was serendipitous, as President Trump was holding a rally there that Ben Domenech wanted me to cover it for the *Federalist*; as it turned out, it would be the first and last indoor Trump rally since the controversial June rally in Tulsa, Oklahoma, an event at which some people believe Herman Cain contracted the virus he would eventually die from, though there is no certain way to prove that. I was anxious to see how the city was doing and talk to the residents about their experiences.

Upon my arrival in Sin City, everything started going wrong; it was like an avalanche of mishap. I am well known as a hapless traveler, like the time I left my laptop at the gate at LAX on my way back to New York City. There was also the time, just back in February, when I forgot to bring my laptop from home to New Hampshire; that was the last Trump rally I covered until Vegas, and I had to write my piece from the press pit on my phone, much to the amusement of other journalists.

But this was much worse. I arrived at the Luxor hotel and casino to promptly realize I had left my phone in the cab. A phone call later from the concierge desk and that was good and sorted, but then I tried to check in. I had left my credit card at home and only had my ATM card. That would have been OK, but I'd had it so long my name and card number had rubbed off. Long story short, I wasn't getting a room. Not there, not anywhere on the strip. Possibly not anywhere in the city. It was a lesson in the decline of the power of cash. I told the guy at the Luxor I'd give him $10,000 in cash as a deposit, which only served to make him seem more suspicious. The end result was no dice, so to speak.

It's not a great feeling, carrying your bags, homeless in the hot Nevada sun, I had plenty of money, but it was useless at these hotels. I worked my phone—which, thank God, the cabbie had returned—and found what has to be one of the five sketchiest motels in all of Las Vegas, which I imagine is a very competitive category. But they were willing to take my card, I could smoke (whatever I wanted to) in my rather dilapidated room, and there was a weed dispensary and a taco place across the street. Twenty-five-year-old Dave would have been in paradise, forty-five-year-old Dave, not so much, but was I surprised by my circumstance? Honestly, not in the slightest.

My cab driver had told me that he thought his business was at about 40 percent of usual; this was the highest number I heard from anyone I spoke to. Most people put it a bit lower. Near my motel off of the strip, things looked damn gloomy: homeless sleeping on the sidewalk, open-air drug deals, most of the businesses closed, including a bar with a sign that said "Last Neighborhood Bar in Las Vegas." The weed dispensary and the 7/11 were open, but not much else.

Over the next three days, I would zip back and forth around Vegas, checking out the casinos that were open. I don't really gamble but I wanted to see how they were managing having so many people indoors. The rules were, well, a bit arbitrary. Social distancing was encouraged but not really enforced on the casino floors. Masks were required at all times unless you were drinking or smoking, which, let's face it, that's like telling a heroin addict they aren't allowed to shoot up unless they are feeling antsy.

In the bars, there was no bar; it was cordoned off, and the tables were staggered about ten feet apart from each other. This made my job kind of difficult, actually. Usually in these situations, I am accustomed to cozying up to the bar and working my way into conversations until I can introduce myself and start asking questions. That was out the window. Instead, I made some remarkably awkward approaches but found as usual that people were very nice about it.

Back in April, the mayor of Las Vegas, Carolyn Goodman, had been pretty desperate to open up; she appeared on CNN with Anderson Cooper and it was an incredibly telling interview. Cooper honestly could not have been ruder to her. Each question came with a pained face of disbelief from the CNN anchor that an elected official could be saying something as irresponsible as her desire to open the casinos. He really just didn't care about the economic devastation; Goodman was saying things counter to the wishes of the all-powerful scientists and that was in and of itself cause for her to be humiliated. As it turned out, Las Vegas did not become a dungeon of viral death upon reopening, but as you might imagine, the self-righteous Vanderbilt scion Cooper offered no apology.

By September, it was obvious why officials in Las Vegas had been so desperate to open, even at the partially open level the city had achieved it was clearly suffering. I had planned the trip, which had been Ben's idea the week before as a hybrid work vacation getaway, I figured my mornings could be spent by the pool, reading or writing, evenings in the new Armani suit I had purchased at the soon to be going out of business Century 21 in Bay Ridge for $300 (it's not like anyone was buying suits) and generally just do whatever people do in Vegas.

My credit card kerfuffle changed all that, but ultimately maybe for the better. My motel was the kind where the city might try to house the homeless only for the homeless to say, "I'm good." Maybe not quite that bad, but not good. A stucco square interior, giant mirrors on two walls, a window on the other and one wall dominated by a television that must have dated from about 1996. It was actually a pretty decent place to write; it had no Wi-Fi so fewer distractions, but still, for the first time in a long time, I actually felt unsafe. The door to my room could easily have been popped unlocked by a reasonably stale stick of chewing gum.

Just the first evening, I witnessed a drug deal in the parking lot my window looked onto, also clear evidence of prostitution, and at least one person who appeared to be carrying a gun. On the two occasions when I had to leave and return to the room in a suit, I did so carefully, jacket and tie in my bag, shirt mostly open and untucked. The rest of the time I wore a beat-up sleeveless T shirt, showing off my tat, shorts, and sneakers, trying very hard to simply blend in to the beat-down surroundings fate had placed me in. My biggest fear was a shooting in the parking lot with stray bullets finding my window, but there was nothing much I could do about that so I just smoked a joint, which only served to make me more paranoid.

It wasn't until later that I realized that this had been, in some sense, a blessing. I was aware of a great personal irony regarding the lockdown and me. I was an early and aggressive critic of the strategy, mostly on the grounds that it was doing great harm to vulnerable people, and yet at least financially, it had done me no harm. I had always worked from home, I was writing more for the *Post*, I was doing more TV, and I inked a book deal all more or less as a result of the lockdown. The Oasis Motel reminded me of what others not so fortunate had been going through; for three nights, I felt a compelled insecurity that for many Americans had stretched for months.

The Sunday of the rally was the also the first Sunday of NFL football. I walked about a mile to Circus Circus, a midrange casino not quite on the actual strip, to check out the sports book and watch the Eagles. It was incredibly empty; by the end of the first quarter, I decided to grab a cab to the Wynn. There was only one cab in the line outside the casino and as I approached it, I saw the driver, seat fully reclined, asleep. I was uncertain about the etiquette in this situation, so I gently tapped on the glass until the gentleman awoke and gestured for me to enter. The drive was probably about eight minutes. In that time, the driver told me how he had just gotten out of jail for sixty days after his girlfriend, who was cheating on him, set him up and stole his apartment; he'd been sleeping in the cab. The poor was guy started crying, saying how grateful he was to have work again and how the next time I saw him his condition would be improved. I assured him that I agreed that would be the case and wished him luck. The ride cost about seven bucks, and I told him to keep the twenty. Then I walked into a fancy casino and aside from the half-worn masks, it was like there was barely a lockdown at all.

Here, you could see the Fendi and Gucci shopping bags, men and women in expensive though annoyingly plain and boring Middle American polo-shirted outfits. All smiles and cigars and the rattling jingle of slots and tables. It brought home again the fallacy of the whole, "We are in this together" narrative. For those of us lucky enough to have kept our jobs, who got a $1,200 stimulus we didn't really need, and who had no movie theaters or restaurants to dispose of income at, the shutdown was like a mini boon. There was extra money to spend, and spent it was. Sadly, the Eagles lost to the Washington Red...er, Football Team. Disappointing, but I had a Trump rally to get to get to so I chugged my beer and found a ride.

When I got to Xtreme Manufacturing, I walked up toward the long, snaking line of red-hatted Trumpists. I recalled having covered the rally in February in New Hampshire. Then had there been a cold, annoying rain peppering the crowd; this day, there was a blazing Nevada sun, but neither the rain nor the sweat of this other occasion dampened the moods. Trump rallies are huge parties and everyone has a good time.

I guess I had noted that the rally was to be indoors, but I hadn't given it much thought. I hadn't even discussed it with anyone at the home office. It wasn't until about an hour before the event started that I realized it was an issue. My first clue was the press pit, which was empty. And by empty, I mean there were like four people in about fifty seats. It wasn't until I was interviewing some people in the crowd that one of them showed me something on their phone, "Can you believe these clowns?" he said to me. It was an article from the

Gateway Pundit about how the cable networks were refusing to allow their correspondents into the event out of fear of the Chinese virus.

ABC News's Jon Karl would say a few days later that covering the rally, as I did, was like bringing your family to cover Fallujah, site of deadly battles during the Iraq War. It didn't feel that way to me. It felt more like what I imagine a swap meet feels like, or something like that. At one point prior to Trump taking the stage, the crowd, as they always do, pointed their attention to the press pit to jeer us. I couldn't stop laughing, I wanted to be like, "I'm on your side…" but I just smiled and waved. I think most of them actually knew I was a conservative journalist because I was the only one not wearing a mask.

As it turned out, no major spike in cases or deaths resulted from the rally. Even if that had happened, it would have been difficult to cite it as the source since as I mentioned all over the strip gamblers and bons vivant were yucking it up maskless at casinos. And that is the broader point. The important one. Las Vegas, in fact, all of our cities, could and should have been operative at even fuller capacity. The most vulnerable economically, the poor and destitute in whose midst I had spent several days, obviously took the harshest hit, even in places that only partially locked down for extended periods.

This is not to say that the problems of poverty, homelessness, and addiction didn't exist prior to the pandemic and the lockdown, but it is to say that those problems could not even be remotely addressed by a city and state government spending all of its energy and attention on the virus and the response to it. Much like our school children left to struggle through useless remote learning, the poor were just thrown under the bus, ignored, and the suffering was palpable and tragic.

Chapter 10

❖

Myth 9—Opposition to Lockdown
Was a Fringe Position

Friday, May 15, was the day when I personally realized I had had it with the lockdown. That it needed to end or at least be significantly loosened. The event that triggered it was a short news report about families in New York City lining up in the wee hours of the morning to receive food from a food bank. It's not that I didn't know that was happening already, but seeing these families, knowing what the fear of food insecurity feels like, how horrible it is for yourself much less your children, something inside me snapped.

There is a story from the ancient world that I read as a teenager but have never been able to find since. I thought it was in Herodotus; maybe I just made it up from several sources. I'm not sure. But in any event, a great king is defeated in battle and must watch as his army, family, treasure, everything is paraded in front of him in chains. He maintains the perfect composure befitting an ancient king until at the very end, he sees a meaningless slave girl in shackles; at that sight, he breaks into tears. I always took it to mean in my own life that the mind can protect us from enormous trauma, but in so doing it often leaves us susceptible to a piercing sadness at comparatively small things.

That's how I felt. In an instant, that sadness turned to anger. I knew other states were three weeks into their openings without the devastating effects of the virus that the media had promised us. I knew that there was much more we could do to ease the pain of the unemployed. I rarely write from a place of anger, mainly because I don't tend to think it produces particularly good work. But this was different; this was an exception, and I wrote a column that I knew went too far, that I knew was a fringe position that probably could not be published, but I had to write it anyway.

This is what I wrote (the lightly edited version that was published, anyway):

"Sometimes, a good rant is all a writer can offer. Bear with me.

Last Friday morning, some 3,500 New Yorkers lined up at a Catholic church in Queens to receive free food hours before it even opened, according to the New York Police Department. Catholic Charities has reported a 200 percent increase in demand over the past month and a half.

By prolonging the coronavirus shutdown long after its core mission was accomplished, Gov. Andrew Cuomo and Mayor Bill de Blasio have plunged tens of thousands of New Yorkers into poverty.

It needs to end. Now.

In mid-March, we were told we have to endure a lockdown to ensure that hospitals didn't get overrun. We did. The hospitals were not overwhelmed. We turned the Javits Center into a hospital. We didn't need it. We brought in a giant Navy ship to treat New Yorkers. We didn't need it.

We were told we were moments away from running out of ventilators. We weren't, and now the United States has built so many, we are giving them away to other countries.

Meanwhile, the Big Apple is dying. Its streets are empty.[37] The bars and jazz clubs, restaurants and coffeehouses sit barren. Beloved haunts, storied rooms, perfect-slice joints are shuttered, many for good. The sweat equity of countless small-business owners is evaporating. Instead of getting people back to work providing for their families, our mayor talks about a fantasyland New Deal for the post-coronavirus era.

Open the city. All of it. Right now. Broadway shows, beaches, Yankees games, the schools, the top of the freakin' Empire State building. Everything. New Yorkers have already learned to socially distance. Businesses can adjust. The elderly and infirm can continue to be isolated.

For two months, we have waited for Cuomo and de Blasio to tell us how this ends. Where is ex-Mayor Michael Bloomberg with his alleged army of tracers that the governor told us was the key to reopening? And why did he hand that responsibility over to Bloomberg, whom nobody elected anyway?

What the hell is going on? Is anybody in charge of this situation? Or are we just left with the governor and his talking-head brother arguing on CNN about which of the two Ma loves best? (Who cares?)

In late April, Georgia Gov. Brian Kemp defied experts by opening his state.[38] The Atlantic magazine, once a serious publication that should now come with a stick of stale bubblegum, accused him of engaging in "human sacrifice."[39]

You want to guess what happened? Guess, come on, take a guess. Instead of the predicted spike in deaths, the number of cases of coronavirus and associated deaths declined.

We should always consider that we are led by idiots, as one of my friends likes to remind me. Cuomo and de Blasio have no plan. There is not a single question about when New York can get back to normal to which they have a straight -

answer. Not one. They cash their taxpayer paychecks while immiserating the rest of us.

If our elected leaders won't save the world's greatest city from a slow death by economic strangulation, then the people of New York must do it themselves. Barbers, tailors, nail - salons, sporting goods stores, movie theaters and others should open their doors—while maintaining social distancing, of course—and dare the state to shut them down.

Our politicians serve by our consent; we don't run our businesses or live our lives by their consent. The suggestion to the contrary is an affront to Americanism.

It has been a long time since this country, let alone this city, really had to deal with the prospect of mass starvation. This isn't about the stock market—it's about parents putting their kids to bed hungry and hoping tomorrow there will be something for them to eat if they get up at 4:30 a.m. and get in line at the food bank.

We did what we were asked. We flattened the freakin' curve. There is no longer any reasonable justification for the government to deprive us of our livelihoods. And our rights aren't the government's to grant or take away. They belong to us—the free grant of nature and the God of nature. We're Americans. More than that: New Yorkers, goddammit."

It took me all of about twenty-five minutes; sometimes, it all just pours out as if you are merely some conduit. I wrote it intending to run it at the *Federalist*, which I already thought might have problems with it. I knew what I was calling for was impossible, a huge overreach, but that was part of the point: our city had been shuttered with broad strokes, nearly total lockdown. Thus far, resisters had asked for bits and pieces back. I was done with that; my offer was this: "Everything. Open everything," then maybe it could be negotiated into some compromise.

I was about to go into the *Federalist*'s back end and start filing it when I had a thought. Obviously, it was a very New York piece, so I figured I would shoot it to Sohrab Ahmari, my editor at the *New York Post*, and see if he wanted it. I was almost certain he would not. In fact, I was absolutely certain that he would not. If I was worried that the *Federalist* might think I was going too far, it was absolutely way too far for the oldest continuous daily newspaper in America. I even said in the email that I knew that, but just wanted to see what he thought anyway.

I was annoyed when it took Sohrab several hours to get back to me since I was so sure he would pass and I was ready to get it up with us. But when Sohrab did get back to me, he said that he thought he could use it early the next week as an online-only piece. That surprised me and was my first indication that maybe I wasn't the only person who shared and was willing to go public with what were, at the time, my very extreme views on the matter.

I didn't really think about it after that until Tuesday afternoon when I received a phone call from Sohrab while I was playing *Rocket League* with Charlie. He was very excited and he said, "It's not 100 percent, but it looks like you've got the wood tomorrow." I informed him I had no idea what that meant. Apparently, in journalistic lingo, "the wood" means the cover. I said something like "That's cool," but I could tell he did not think I was sufficiently excited. I thought he meant that my story would be on a banner, or some cutaway part of the cover. It wasn't really until he sent me a photo of the finished cover with the note, "This is the one you frame for your grandkids" that I really understood what was happening.

The entire cover of the *New York Post* was a picture of the New York skyline with a giant headline reading "IT NEEDS TO END NOW" with an excerpt from the story below it. *The New York Post* was not just running my piece; it was endorsing it. For arguably the first time since the lockdown began, a major news organization was challenging what could not be challenged, was demanding we get our lives back regardless of what the scientists said. I was excited, of course, but also nervous. I wasn't nervous that I would be dragged by the Left and some on the Right for penning such an "irresponsible" piece; I was nervous that by questioning the shibboleths of virus prevention, I may actually hurt people. That some may read my work, which by then I knew would go viral like nothing I had ever written before, and neglect the rules in place meant to make them safe.

For months, I had struggled along with other journalists skeptical of the lockdown with this fear. What if I was wrong? What if Dave Marcus, who is not a scientist and never even played one on TV (though I did once in a play), was giving people a green light to put themselves in danger? But what I realized was that I was making myself out to be too important. Millions of Americans were already making choices that, according to scientists, put themselves and others at risks. I wasn't the one moving public opinion and behavior so much as public opinion and behavior was moving me.

But I was still nervous about it in terms of potentially getting people hurt. I thought I was right, and I knew people were getting hurt by the lockdowns anyway, but it's still morally scary when you are advising something that a bunch of scientists say will literally get people killed. And I wasn't alone. Around this time, Tucker Carlson was also starting to question and I asked him about that.

"I was calling for everything to open, right? And yeah, I did that for certain reasons. I wanted to take the most extreme position to push the conversation more to the middle. You were also starting to question the lockdown, which, at that point, not just me and you, people like Bethany Mandel, anybody who violated the scientific guidance, that was killing Grandma. How difficult a choice was that for you guys, when you started going out on that limb?"

"It wasn't hard at all. I mean, we're just by pure luck, living in this perfect world journalistically, where we never get any, and I mean literally any, interference with our editorial line. No one's ever said 'You've got to say this. You can't say that,' not one time in eleven years in the Fox Network, so that's an unusual place to be. I think the real reason; it's the personal courage of the guys who own the company. But it's also the fact that we're not dependent on Google and Facebook for traffic. So it wasn't really scary for us at all. What was scary was to see people submit to unreasonable commands that were political rather than science based, and I just never, I mean, that's a really stressing thing. It's not that politicians took advantage of a crisis to increase their power. OK, what do you think they were going to do? It's that the public didn't fight back."

He hadn't quite answered my question, so I pushed a bit. "So, when you started questioning the efficacy of the lockdowns, as an individual, did you have any fear or trepidation in terms of the fact that you might be giving people bad advice, we could get them hurt?"

"Of course. I've worried about that since the beginning. I mean, I've supported all kinds of things, including abortion, that I'm horrified that I supported. And because the nature of my job is to express an opinion on television, some number of people, they believe you. So, yes, that that's something I worry about every single day. We were very cautious about putting out Alex Berenson on at first, for example."

"Yep."

"Because he's a novelist who was a *New York Times* reporter, no, he doesn't have a medical degree, is not properly credentialed. And it's hard for me to assess some of the claims. So we were very careful, very careful about getting over our skis. And I've kept every, I wrote all the scripts, and I've kept them all. Not because we're worried about getting sued or something, but because we won't be good citizens."

"Yeah, he's done great work."

Everyone I spoke to who expressed opposition to the lockdowns told me the same thing: that there was fear of giving bad information, especially when those on the other side were so absolute in their condemnation. But in a way, that absolutism only strengthened the convictions of those challenging the response. The other side's refusal to even entertain the demonstrable downsides of the shutdown made making that case even more important.

The *Post* puts its op-eds up online about 6 p.m. the night before it runs, and in cases like this, also its cover. The reaction was immediate. My Twitter feed became a useless fast-moving ticker tape of mostly positive reaction that I couldn't keep up with. Eventually, I just shut it down, hung out with my kid, and went to sleep, knowing the next day would be a big one.

By the time I opened my laptop at 7 a.m., I already had media requests, mostly from Fox News. I turned on Fox News and in segment after segment, the cover appeared with a slew of guests commenting most in either partial or full support. That afternoon, Rush Limbaugh read the piece in its entirety to his millions of listeners. You would always know when Rush referenced you because people would start texting you all excited about it; it is evidence of the man's extraordinary reach. Sebastian Gorka also read it on his show, which was my favorite; his dulcet, accented voice made it sound like some cross between a children's story and an angry screed.

The reaction to the piece, both from the media and from civilians, shocked me. Sen. Chuck Schumer would be asked about it and insist that he didn't take orders from tabloids, but some kind of wave was breaking in the tide of public opinion.

About two months later, the *Federalist* had a boot camp in DC for our summer crop of interns. Most of the poor kids had been slated to spend the whole summer in the capital, but the lockdown diminished that to a long weekend. As the only member of senior staff who is not an editor (thank God. I want no part of any of that—I mean, so many emails, I imagine—it makes me shudder) I was tasked with doing the lecture on op-ed writing.

After playing the kids some Kerouac off of my laptop and telling them to "Try to write like that," I gave them a piece of advice I learned from the cover story. Columnists get knocked for not being reporters; we bring heat, not light, it is said. There are too many of us, the news is too opinion driven, blah, blah, blah. But there is something very important that only a columnist can really do, and it might be our most import function. Sometimes, there is an opinion held by many, maybe even most people, that nobody feels comfortable saying. They believe it; they think it's true, but societal pressure makes them keep mum about it. If a columnist can find that opinion, the one just below the surface, ready, volcanolike, to explode, they can free others to say what was forbidden before. That is exactly what happened.

It had taken two months, two months of slavishly following the science, even when guidance changed (such as with masks), even when the collateral damage of lockdown was piling up in huge, tragic mounds, but all of that was about to change. Conservative media would never go back to a sheepish acknowledgment that lockdowns and the science behind them must not be challenged. The conversations from March about how to responsibly cover this story had given way to the skepticism that should always be the natural position of the news media.

And that was really it, right? Skepticism. Giving facts and opinions to the American people and allowing them to decide. Objective journalism is like objective truth: a fine idea, perhaps, but rarely ever seen in practice. What if, in fact, we were not hearing the whole story? What if there were still subjective judgments for the people to make? What if there were voices, even in the scientific community, being ignored or shunned because they challenged the narrative? What if social media companies and Google were actively trying to suppress legitimate ideas to protect the "health" and "safety" of the conversation? Insidious terms these that strike at the heart of free speech. Oh sure, you can say whatever you want, so long as it is not "unhealthy." What if, as Dr. Fauci would admit in December, he was basing what he chose to tell the American people and keep from the American people based on polling and public opinion? Put bluntly, what if we were being treated like children?

The following weekend was Memorial Day weekend, a major test of the American people's willingness to stay locked down. And in some cases, Republican political leaders like Texas Gov. Greg Abbott would begin reducing the restrictions to allow for people to gather and celebrate the onset of summer. The *Washington Post* put it this way, "…traffic was backed up for miles in Corpus Christi, Tex., as people traveled to Padre Island's beaches. Texas Gov. Greg Abbott (R) moved the state into Phase 2 of reopening Monday, which among other changes allows restaurants to increase their occupancy to 50 percent. Bars were allowed to open Friday."

In New York City, the beaches would be open with a smattering of strange rules and regulations. They could only be full to 50 percent capacity (I had no idea that beaches actually had official capacities, but whatever); there could be no swimming, for some reason. I remember thinking Bill de Blasio was a bit like Lucille Bluth in *Arrested Development* telling Buster "You are not swimming in the ocean!" But unlike Texas, in Gotham, restaurants and bars would have to wait another four months to open their doors.

Cable news was awash in horror over pool parties and in Ocean City, New Jersey, boardwalks crushed with throngs as dogged reporters counted masks and judged how many feet apart the corn dog and funnel cake-consuming beach goers were from each other. For his part, Dr. Fauci was all for some outdoor exercise for people weary of being shut up at home, as CNN reported on May 23: ""Go out, wear a mask, stay 6 feet away from anyone so you can have the physical distancing," he told a CNN Coronavirus town hall. "Go for a run. Go for a walk. Go fishing. As long as you're not in a crowd and you're not in a situation where you can physically transmit the virus."

What was starting to happen was unfortunate, and frankly, I think I was guilty of it to some degree. Rather than meeting somewhere in the middle between lockdowns and masking on the one hand and open economies and limited restrictions on the other, both sides became entrenched in more extreme positions. For me, this was a conscious choice, though one not taken lightly, and in some ways, it reflected the logic of the other side of the debate as well. My purpose in calling for total opening, for an absolute return to normal for almost all of the population was not realistic, but rather meant to push those in favor of lockdowns closer to the middle, to some kind of reasonable opening.

This is not entirely unlike those lockdown advocates, especially in the media, who would brook no doubts about the efficacy of the harmful halting of the American economy. They also seemed to understand on some level their militant orthodoxy in all things Covid was at least partially performance meant to frighten the population into obeying as many of the measures as possible, all while understanding that to some significant degree, people would make their own choices. This is why we saw pictures of maskless Nancy Pelosi at the hair salon. It also explains how CNN's Chris Cuomo, the most supposedly pious of the Coronavirus high priests, wound up being scolded by his own building manager for not following masking protocols.

This was all hypocrisy, of course, but of a special kind. Almost everyone negotiated in their own minds between projecting the proper attitude of concern and care out onto the world while trusting themselves to pick and choose the regulations responsibly. And that cuts to the heart of the matter: we trust ourselves more than we trust others. Politically, that was also becoming the focus point of debate: how much of the pandemic response should be voluntary, from the people, and how much compelled and enforced by the state?

Meanwhile, at this point in late May, cases and deaths were rising in the states like Florida, Georgia, and Colorado that had chosen to be more open, but not by anywhere near the staggering numbers that the naysayers and doomsday crowd with their mantra of "just wait two weeks" promised would occur. The nation was poised for a new debate about how to fight the pandemic. It was a move away from panic; the staggering death tolls of April were behind us, at least until winter; a new way might have been needed. But we won't ever actually know how that would have turned out. Instead, something else happened. Something that nobody could have actually expected. The entire debate about lockdowns, in fact a broader debate about America herself, was about to change. Unbeknownst to us, America's deadly virus was about to crash headlong into America's oldest sin.

Chapter 11

Myth 10—The Virus Can't Spread at Antiracism Protests

It is at once entirely amazing and entirely predictable that the activity that came to defy all of the usual rules that had been established for the lockdown was the protesting of antiblack racism and police brutality. Nothing else beyond the most basic needs of medicine and food had been considered important enough to allow large gatherings, even outdoors, even with masks. But fighting racism was different and it is vitally important to understand why.

George Floyd died in Minneapolis on May 25. The killing was not a police shooting, but rather reminiscent of the killing of Eric Garner by the New York Police Department; it resulted from a police officer kneeling on Floyd's neck for eight minutes. Floyd later died. The actions of that officer and of the three others with him that day were almost universally condemned on all sides; indeed, what we could see from the video taken by bystanders seemed indefensible. Like Garner, Floyd said, "I can't breathe," and he also called out to his dead mother. In the ensuing months, more context would emerge and as of writing this, the murder case against the officers is still pending, but in the days following Floyd's death, nuance was not on most people's minds.

As crowds began to gather in the afternoon daylight of the Twin Cities, the implication was obvious to everyone immediately. Throughout April and May, beachgoers and pool party attendees across the country had been cracked down upon and scolded for their selfishness in gathering despite the risk of spreading the Chinese virus. Even protests like those in Michigan against the lockdown were viewed this way by most of the corporate media, although tellingly, law enforcement did little to break up the crowds. It was yet another example of the lockdown that was barely ever enforced. For the most part, it didn't have to be. The antilockdown protests had gotten their message out; they may have even had a lot of support, but it was not enough to convince masses of people to defy the state. Also importantly, governors of locked-down states had strong sticks to keep businesses from opening. From fines to loss of liquor licenses, the power of the state was too much to be resisted.

As soon as the Floyd protests started, they were viewed through a political lens in very different ways by our two Americas. The Left and most of the corporate media were frankly in a bind. For months, they had been insisting that these exact kinds of gatherings were basically the equivalent of murder, and yet owing to a decade long buildup of racial tension and new ways of thinking about what racism is, they were essentially forbidden by the new rules of race from criticizing the protests.

The reason for this is that the American Left had come to accept and to import from the academy, the arts, the media, and increasingly woke corporations a new definition of racism that was at odds with the traditional definition still used generally by those on the Right. That traditional definition holds that racism is a belief or an action, that it requires one to have animosity toward a racial group, or at least to believe that racial groups and individuals in those groups are inherently superior or inferior. Most importantly, the traditional definition of racism requires intent; it is something you actively and knowingly do. It is something you do, not something you are. From this perspective, the efficacy of protests, and certainly of violence and looting in fighting racism, is dubious. The civil rights movement of the 1950s and 1960s had been focused on changing laws and actual policies that stood in the way of black achievement. By our own time, such directly racist laws had been all but expunged from the dusty rows of law books. Racism now needed to be shown to be an irrational personal failing; the power lies with the individual.

Critical race theory, from which the new progressive definition of racism emerged, turned all of this accepted wisdom on its head. No, it argued, racism is not about intent or individual actions; it is a system of oppression that operates even without the knowledge of those engaged in it. The concept of white privilege had been established to attempt to show that even without knowing it, white people were engaging in racism with nearly every breath. Peggy McIntosh introduced this theory to the world in the late 1980s with a pamphlet-sized screed called "White Privilege: Unpacking the Invisible Knapsack."

The basic concept here is that in a whole host of ways, whiteness is considered the norm in our society and white people interact with our society without a whole host of problems faced by blacks. These included not being followed in stores out of fear of stealing, seeing more people who look like you in the workplace or in entertainment, and an almost endless supply of others. But the bottom line, the most important point, was that this was a kind of racism one can be guilty of without even knowing it. This was important because prior to the emergence of critical race theory, our culture had labored under the notion that the problems of racism were getting better, and fast. After all, if you were fifty years old in 1980, you had been born while people who were slaves still lived, been an adult during segregation, seen the civil rights movement, and landed in a place that seemed vastly more equal than any of that. Few, if any, people in 1986 would have said racism didn't exist, but the progress was palpable and undeniable.

In 1986, for example, *The Cosby Show* was the most popular show on television, but more than that, the Huxstables, the family at the core of the show, were the absolute model of a successful American family. They were a black, two-professional-parent household living comfortably in a middle-class, multicultural Brooklyn neighborhood in which everyone seemed to get along. If this black family being the lodestar American family didn't signal a shift away from racism, then what would?

Just three years later, in 1989, another smash hit would break through in American entertainment. Film director Spike Lee's *Do the Right Thing* was set in the same multicultural Brooklyn as *The Cosby Show*, but now there was a simmering cauldron of racial tension lying just beneath the surface. The movie introduced us to another key element of critical race theory, "the microaggression." After all, the "racist act" that sets the plot in motion toward its final moments of riots and police killing a black man was that Sal's Pizza didn't have any pictures of black entertainers on the wall, only Italians.

In a seminal scene, we see close-up after close up of Brooklynites of various races hurling racial epithets. The message is clear; we were still essentially a racist society. Yes, we had learned to be more polite, less overt; we had gone from Archie Bunker feeling comfortable being openly racist in the 1970s to such open sentiments being a fireable offense in our society. Cases like Jimmy the Greek, the CBS football analyst, and many others saw powerful men cancelled, though we did not have that term yet.

Importantly, to be credibly accused of racism was a capital offense in the sense that one's reputation could scarcely recover from it. But there was a transaction at work in this. In order for racism to be punished so severely, it had to be proven beyond a reasonable doubt. If the result was to be that a person could never work again, then the accusation itself had to be so clear, so unambiguous that the punishment fit the crime. If, on the other hand, we are all somewhat vaguely racist, at least white people anyway, that cannot be dealt with by firing hundreds of millions of Americans. Some other means, like reparations or racial sensitivity training, had to take the place of universal permanent condemnation.

It took several decades for critical race theory, which has roots dating back from the 1990s, and even further back to the "psychological wage" concept of WEB Dubois, to become the dominant mode of talking and thinking about racism in the American media. It began in the academy, and by the late 1990s, has moved in to the nonprofit art world, where as a theater artist and producer, I saw its grip on discourse become firmer year after year. By the 2010s, it had moved to social media, where memes about privilege abounded and CRT crashed into the mainstream mostly on the back of college-educated white progressives who emerged as by far the most progressive cohort of Americans, eclipsing even any groups of color.

So by the time the protests broke out, the corporate media already existed in a landscape where any criticism of these demands for racial justice would be wildly problematic. Excuses had to be made for them and were; even epidemiologists contorted themselves into nonscientific pretzels to defend "the work" of dismantling systemic racism and the attack on black and brown bodies, as the CRT rhetoric puts it. An argument emerged that said that since racism is also a public health crisis, like the virus itself, then fighting the one offset the danger of the other. But not everyone was convinced.

The night of the first protest, everyone at the *Federalist* had the very same reaction, as did everyone on the journalist WhatsApp list. That's it, we all thought. This has to be over now. There was no way that anyone could justify continuing with the lockdown as it was then while condoning protest gatherings of thousands, even tens of thousands, we naively believed. There was almost a sense of gratitude; it was not that we agreed with everything the protesters were saying, and we certainly did not condone the rioting, arson, looting, and murder that was evident even in those early nights of violence, but we were frankly glad that more people were standing up and refusing to be locked down.

Earlier, I referenced a conversation with Glenn Loury on how we should not give our democracy over to unelected scientists, but I didn't give you the whole quote. He said when I asked if he was shocked by the media giving a pass to the protests,

"These are public health experts that have urged us on the basis of models and projections of hundreds of thousands or millions of people being killed that we had to shut down everything, OK? These were the very same people who said 'follow the science, follow the science, follow the science.' They decided to declare that racism is also a public health threat, and therefore if you were out there protesting racism with the prospect that you might reduce antiblack racism, you were contributing to public health to the extent that it was worth risking spreading the virus. Now if that's not a paper-thin, transparent, tendentious, absurd, and politically biased argument, I don't what it is."

Indeed. There was agitation and aggravation in Loury's voice; he was talking to me via Zoom about two months after the protests and rioting started and still we lived in the bizarre world in which filling Yankee Stadium at quarter capacity for a baseball game was absolutely forbidden, with no real plan for when it might not be, but the same elected officials banning it were applauding, sometimes even marching with the protesters. As more scientists and media types continued babbling the same nonsense about how this was all justified because racism was a public health crisis as severe as Covid, or saying, but "Hey look, they are mostly wearing masks, so…" anger began to build among those not aligned with the protests.

One person who felt that anger, and who became a touchstone for others feeling it was Fox News weather analyst Janice Dean. Dean had lost both her father and mother-in-law to Covid months earlier. Her desperate tale about her family not being able to see and care for these loved ones in their final days and not being to properly mourn them resonated with thousands and thousands of Americans who experienced a similar depravation; when it came to the people they lost, their deaths didn't matter.

Dean told me that seeing the protests, she thought, "It felt like we were in upside-down world. I received more comments during that time. My gosh, thousands of people are gathering and we still could not have not a wake or funeral. We can't do what we are supposed to do. It made the grief that much harder."

Once again, the great tagline of the lockdown was "We are all in this together." Once again, it proved to be a cruel fiction; those like me who had jobs that let them work from home, income steady, rent paid, food on the table experienced a lockdown of inconvenience; those who worked in shuttered industries like retail, food service, or entertainment were, on the other hand, facing existential threats. But those disparities were the diktat of science and public policy experts; they were supposedly not subjective but the result of hard science and numbers. As protesters filled the streets not only in Minneapolis, but in Brooklyn and Chicago, and Portland and Seattle, a different kind of disparity was coming into sharp focus.

This was a disparity of ideology, in some sense, a disparity of religion. If your religion was Christianity, or Judaism, or Islam, you were still forbidden in many cases from even outdoor, socially distanced services for your congregation. But if your religion was the woke new faith of critical race theory, if you put your faith in skin color as the metaphysical defining factor of who you and others are, and what your place in the society is, well, that church was open for business. The thousands thronged the streets, some true believers, some just curious; others frankly came because it was basically the only thing they were allowed to do. All the bread and circuses had been cancelled except this one. And amazingly, this protest exemption, this special dispensation, would linger for weeks, even codified in government orders across the country. It is truly one of the most remarkable and disturbing social phenomena of the entire lockdown experience. But it happened.

Nobody I work with believed at first that these kinds of large-scale gatherings could be not only allowed, but be cheered while the lockdown rules of the previous weeks remained fully in place. It had been less than two weeks since my *Post* cover ran, but even before the protests started, steam was being gained for broader reopening and in much of the country, as we saw with Georgia and Florida, that was already happening. Every conservative outlet in the country ran some version, "OK, this is over now, right?" But of course it wasn't. Not the protesting, not the rioting, not the lockdown.

What was so galling about the situation, especially in terms of the media, but also from elected officials' reaction, was the utter unwillingness to simply be honest. In a frankly weird statement more than a month after the protests began New York City, mayor Bill de Blasio said of them, "That is something that again transcends all normal realities because we are at a moment of history when that had to be said and done; that's a decision I made." What? What the hell does, "transcends all normal realities," mean? See what I'm saying? I wasn't kidding when I called it a religion; after all what else do you call a set of beliefs that transcends all normal realities?

One of the most bizarre and flummoxing decisions made during and in the wake of the protest was when authorities in New York City charged with contact tracing were told not to ask if people testing positive for Covid had attended protests. Tracers were told not to proactively ask about it, but rather just have people volunteer that they had been to protests if they so chose.

These were by far the largest public gatherings of any kind in New York City since the lockdown began. It was exactly the kind of event that officials had warned about as a potential superspreader event. Even if many people were masked, they were also yelling and screaming. It's one ridiculous thing to allow these events to take place while all others are banned, but it is insane to then decide that the government won't actively develop data to determine how much spread had been caused by them. If nothing else, the opportunity to study in so much detail the impact of large, dense, outdoor gatherings could have provided us with much-needed insight on how and when other such gatherings could take place. For that reason alone, attention should have been paid. So why on earth would the authorities ignore this opportunity?

The answer is not entirely clear. In the wake of the decision, New York City reported that "Jonah Bruno, an [New York State Health Department] agency spokesperson, stated, 'We're working with New York City to balance the public health priority while also protecting personal privacy, as we seek to ensure a thorough contact tracing program that helps us contain the COVID-19 virus and monitor any fluctuations in the infection rate as we continue reopening New York.'"

Now, wait a minute, asking people to list every individual they have been in close contact with is not an invasion of personal privacy, but asking them if they attended a massive public protest is? Was there some paranoid fear that if the government had a list of people who had protested, they could use it at some point for nefarious means? Even though the government itself was fully in support of those protests? And if so, should people be worried that the state might eventually use the information they gathered about individuals for nefarious purposes? It was yet another double standard that made absolutely no sense.

For more than two months, the only reality that existed in America was the spread of the virus; almost every aspect of almost everyone's life was shut down to confront this reality.

Now of a sudden, it was transcended? Now, a leaderless movement that included not just peaceful protest but arson, looting, and eventually murder, that seemed to have the absurd goal of abolishing the police was so important that the virus could be ignored? This truly was the moment when the charade was revealed; we knew right then just how much of the lockdown had been politically motivated because our leaders and media were telling us so. All of the lies became obvious, of course; this was political, they were lies, they were lies. They were lies.

But there were further lies, deeper and more obvious ones, that emerged in this furious season of gaslighting. The morning after looting and arson ravaged Minneapolis, officials including Minnesota Attorney General Keith Ellison would assert, more or less baselessly, that they believed that the violence was the work of white supremacists infiltrating the otherwise peaceful protest. Let's be clear: this is not true; it was never true. Although there were straggling Boogaloo Boys or ne'er-do-wells out for kicks fanning the flames, the vast majority of the violence was committed by those actually protesting against the police. But we weren't supposed to know that, just as we weren't supposed to know that the economic and human cost of the lockdown was devastating the country.

What nobody really expected at the beginning of June was just how long these protests and riots would continue. In the first week or so, there was a sense that they could peter out. It was, after all, something that we had seen before: a few days of clashes, it quiets down, and then things go back to normal until the next time. But this had never happened during a pandemic lockdown before, and with little else for people to do, the protests grew not only in the United States but in Europe as well. All over the world, masses of people were gathering to demand that the Minneapolis Police Department reform and/or that the officers involved in the death of Floyd be arrested, which did indeed happen. But that also did not stop the protests.

In this sense, and in several others, the protests resembled the Occupy Wall Street movement of 2011. That was also a leaderless movement, although it did have a rough governing system called the General Assembly, in which policies and plans would be voted on, usually requiring a consensus, using up twinkles and down twinkles, a kind of signal made with one's hands. The biggest knock on Occupy at first was that it was entirely unclear what concrete changes they were asking for. Yes, they wanted corporate money out of politics, and in general a crackdown on capitalism at least as currently practiced. But again, without a leadership system, the movement failed to produce an actionable agenda. In fact, they didn't just fail; they didn't even try.

This was excused at the time by most in the corporate media. Who cares, they argued, if Occupy Wall Street had concrete plans and ideas; they were starting a conversation or something. Young people were finally rising up in an organic way to protest economic inequality. In actuality, it was not so organic; it was organized by groups such as the Canadian progressive magazine *Ad Busters*, and whatever conversation they started never made it to Barack Obama's White House. Just five years after the dust settled at the Occupation's home at Zuccotti Park in lower Manhattan, Donald Trump would win the presidency. Now, a new occupation had arisen all over the country, some literal like the doomed CHOP in Seattle, some looser, like the nights of violence that would rock Philadelphia months later in October.

The politics of this were not just racial but also presidential. A calculation was made by Democrats that the unrest, with its allegations of racism, played badly for President Trump. Being on the side of the protesters made sense for most Democrats, notwithstanding the obvious hypocrisy of the moment. Kamala Harris, who was on the shortlist to be the vice presidential nominee, went all in, urging her Twitter followers to donate funds to the Minnesota Bail Fund to get the protesters, or rioters depending on your view,

195

out of jail. Several Biden campaign officials as well as big name Hollywood celebrities donated to the fund. Although this rather undermined the idea that the violence was caused by white supremacists; after all, why would those unsung heroes, Hollywood celebrities, bail out Neo-Nazis?

Months later, this would become a negative campaign issue for Biden, but at the time, his campaign just rode the zeitgeist of the moment into what looked like an obvious winning choice. And it wasn't just Biden. In New York City, the race for Congress in its only swing district the New York 11th seemed like a comfortable race for Max Rose, who had flipped it blue in 2018. But as the election grew nearer, and chaos and violence ran through the nation, his appearance at an antipolice rally in Staten Island in June would come to define a tightening campaign with his back-the-blue opponent Nicole Malliotakis. Like Trump, she would garner all of the police endorsements, and she would eventually dispatch the otherwise moderate Rose.

This new battle over narrative would last months. As violence and rioting spread on the Left, eventually especially focused on Antifa, a shadowy movement most Americans knew little about. The Democrats would continue to insist that there was violence on both sides, that Antifa, in the words of Rep. Jerrold Nadler, "is a myth," and the protests were "mostly peaceful." "We are all in this together." But now another dimension of difference emerged. Half of the country seemed inspired by the brave protesters, risking themselves and others to the ravages of the virus in the name of racial justice, and the other half was furious after being told to essentially halt their lives that these groups of hooligans were destroying property and tearing statues with what appeared to be the full blessing of our betters, who had locked us all in our houses about ten minutes earlier.

There was perhaps no better example than the statues. What had started a few years earlier as attempts to take down monuments to Confederate generals devolved into a free-for-all of destruction that lacked any discernable rhyme or reason. Statues of abolitionists, statues of Ulysses S. Grant, George Washington, and even of a Catholic saint fell. The Museum of Natural History in New York City announced that its famous equestrian statue of Theodore Roosevelt would come down; in Ohio, a statue of Christopher Columbus was removed by the city of, well, Columbus. The lockdown had moved into a new iconoclastic stage. I'm not sure anyone had that on their pandemic bingo card.

There just didn't seem to be any rules, and there also was no real leadership structure among the protesters that could maintain order and create a movement more like the civil rights movement. The death of an icon of those times, Congressman John Lewis, would put a fine point on this headless hydra of mass protest. The seminal image of Lewis is of him leading a march across the Edmund Pettus Bridge in March of 1965; he and his followers would be attacked on what became known as Bloody Sunday. What moved the nation so much was that the protestors remained peaceful as the police attacked them. That perhaps more than anything else helped to galvanize Americans around the movement.

But nothing even remotely like Bloody Sunday took place during the 2020 riots. In Seattle, police simply gave up one of their buildings to protestors and allowed them to set up the autonomous zone known as CHOP. This again amounted to a large gathering that would have otherwise been legally prohibited. The best the media and Democrats could come up with as to why this was even remotely OK was again the claim that most of them were wearing masks, but even with masks, gatherings like CHOP were banned all over the country. One could even reasonably wonder in retrospect if the almost talismanic power of masks that so many insisted upon was, in some measure, a result of the need to give antiracism a pass on their protests.

Seattle's mayor, Jenny Durkan, predicted when this all started that it might well turn into a "Summer of Love." Instead, two people were murdered in the occupied zone before finally the mayor had had enough and shut it down not long after police chief Carmen Best, a black woman leading the Seattle police force, would resign in frustration at a city government that would not let her do her job. And yet still the Seattle City Council voted in favor of draconian cuts to the police; it was mind-boggling. And when it was pointed out that the jobs that would be cut in the department would be those of the newer and more racially diverse officers, the council simply tried to find ways to impose racial guidelines as to who should be fired. Fighting racism suddenly meant firing people because of the color of their skin, an irony that seemed utterly lost on most of the media.

In New York City, police were told to use a "light touch" even as "protesters" in Brooklyn threw Molotov cocktails into police cars and wide swaths of Manhattan were looted. I remember when the violence hit Brooklyn; Ben Domenech called me to check in and offered his and his wife Meghan McCain's apartment in a fortress-like building in Midtown Manhattan to Libby, Charlie, and me if things got bad. I really was very grateful, but I assured Ben that with the number of cops who live in Bay Ridge, it might just be the safest place in the city. And if that failed, there was also the last resort of the mafia. Should they rioters have ventured into South Brooklyn, they might have found a situation where "Now youse can't leave."

The strange thing was these protests were ostensibly about police brutality and in at least some of the cases that caused charged reactions there had seemed to be malfeasance. But at the same time, they were isolated incidents, and again, in dealing with the protesters, there was little to no violence. There were a handful of incidents, but far more incidents of police showing remarkable restraint when attacked by rioters. Even when not attacked physically, they endured an incredible degree of verbal abuse, often racially tinged and directed at officers of color. And yet there seemed nobody on the Left willing to say, "Hey, knock that off. I support what you are fighting for but this isn't acceptable."

One thing that really wasn't happening during this period of violent protest was any serious attempt to address the underlying conditions that lead to police brutality. The answer from the far Left seemed to be to defund or even abolish the police; on the Right, there was massive support for police and perhaps even a bit of dismissiveness about there really being a problem. But as a result of the lockdown, much of the regular business of local government, including attempts at police reform, were simply not able to be dealt with. In a New York State effectively being run as a Cuomo dictatorship, for example, how could real solutions make their way through a normal and thorough political process? Put simply, they could not be. Like almost everything else, effective governance was put on hold.

In cities and states across America, even in the summer, governors and mayors had many if not most of the emergency powers that had been granted them in March. This was in no way, shape, or form conducive to a productive overview and reform of police forces. Our governments simply were not operating in the manner they are meant to. As with so much else, the new emergency structure of the political landscape was justified by and entirely motivated by Covid response. The machinery of the state that in normal times makes meaningful reform happen was out of commission. Emergency powers are not meant to bring about careful, examined, long-term solutions; they are about getting through tomorrow or next week. But with these powers almost set in stone, substantive change simply was not happening.

As June slowed to an end, much of America was on fire, one set by the new radicals. Meanwhile, though, with the exception of a brief but sharp spike of deaths on or around June 25, the totals of sometimes two thousand-plus deaths a day in April and early May would not be reached again until the onset of winter.

At this time, Pew released a poll asking people if they thought that the worst of the virus was behind us or still to come. When asked this in April, majorities of both Democrats and Republicans agreed the worst was still to come, 87 percent of the former said this, 56 percent of the latter. But by June, only 38 percent of Republicans thought the worst was yet to come, and yet 76 percent of Democrats still held that view. Purely in terms of deaths, it is hard to say which group wound up being right. In the winter, deaths would again reach the highs of spring nationally, but in a way that was much more spread out across the country. But it really didn't matter. Democrats were still living in fear of the virus and would for months to come—Republicans, far less so.

By October, this gap would become even more dramatic; in one Gallup poll, 70 percent of Democratic men and 80 percent of Democratic women were "worried about getting the coronavirus" while only 20 percent of Republican men and 29 percent of Republican women reported the same. Back in March, when all of this was just beginning, there was a partisan division regarding fear of the virus, but it was nowhere near as stark. An NBC/*Wall Street Journal* poll at the time showed that 68 percent of Democrats were worried someone in their family would catch the virus, 40 percent of Republicans were, as were 45 percent of independents. It is fascinating and troubling to note that even as we learned more about the virus, even as the mortality rate dropped significantly, and even as it worked its way through our society, the partisan division regarding it grew; it didn't shrink. There can be few starker measures of just how significantly the two Americas were existing in competing realities.

By July, when the presidential election was moving into full swing, albeit with Joe Biden staying more or less in his house, not out on the campaign trail, the unrest across the country was becoming a major part of the race. In fact, until Election Day, the two issues that would resound most loudly were the handling of the virus and the explosion of anger at perceived antiblack racism in America and in its policing. The conventional wisdom was that this unrest, especially as it made its way into whiter, more suburban areas, would frighten white voters, especially suburban white women, and send them into Trump's camp, and anger minority, especially black, voters to an extent that would reap electoral gains for Joe Biden. As we will see later, this is not exactly what happened, but the reason so many thought that it would had a lot to do with questionable a priori assumptions about race and elections, the basic assumption being, as Joe Biden unartfully put it, that if you didn't vote for him, "you ain't black."

When the virus first hit, we were told again and again that it did not care about politics. But suddenly, when the issue became racism, that wisdom was just thrown out the window. For many Americans, this was a breach of trust that would never be mended. As the summer of discontent gave way to an autumn of elections, the battle lines had been clearly drawn. For those opposed to the lockdown regimes, the pass given to protest would be a potent weapon in their arguments for opening. If the rules could not be enforced equally, they would argue, then they should not be enforced at all.

Chapter 12

---◇---

Myth 11—Conservatives Were
Divided on Trump's Response

By July, it had literally been more than three months since I had attended any form of social occasion outside of hanging out with a few people in my backyard. As protesters were whooping it up in almost every major city in America, disregarding the Coronavirus rules like they were bedtime at a sleepover for ten-year-olds, Sohrab Ahmari had had enough. With his family safely ensconced with relatives in New England, he was ready to throw a party—um…make that a protest. This all had to be done very carefully, of course, along with the city's rules limiting the number of participants in gatherings. Sohrab lives in a co-op, that most awful of housing arrangements in which abject authoritarians on the board create arbitrary rules to confirm and bask in their power. In some sense, it was as if all of New York City had become a restrictive co-op. So there was a cap on attendees, though he was able to wrangle his lovely neighbor Ruth into cohosting, which meant that she could have guests as well, swelling our mass gathering up to about twelve people.

Libby and I went, along with Abe Greenwald from *Commentary*, whom I had never met off of the list beforehand but who is a hell of a nice guy. From the *Post* along with Sohrab were Kelly Jane Torrance and Elisha Maldonado, and there were a few lovely civilian friends of the host as well. To say that I was excited to actually hang out in live person with other human beings and dress up a little and see them dressed up a little too would be the understatement of the lockdown. And at the same time, it felt like one of those early '90s illegal raves where you had to meet a bus at some random location that would take you to the actual rave. It felt dirty and transgressive, which as far as I have ever been able to tell, is exactly what you want from a party.

Part of the fun was Sohrab's paranoia that he would get caught by the building, as we went downstairs to smoke several times it was like *Spy vs. Spy* getting past the doorman, this is why you should never live in a co-op, kids. I kept assuring him that he wasn't breaking the rules; in fact, he was doing a fine service for desperate New Yorkers who had been cooped up like prisoners for months.

With Sohrab's charcuterie laid out, Jason Epstein, a consultant and friend of the New York conservatives complained that it was all pork, to which he was told he was free to eat crackers. Kelly and Elisha arrived; soon, a kitchen table was surrounded by friends, chatting across and over each other. Perhaps the best way to describe it is like the first warm day of spring when you cast off your sweater and feel that palpable remembrance of having felt this before, over and over throughout your life.

I think of the kitchen table in my great-grandfather's house in Philly, much longer than Sohrab's—he did have fifteen kids, after all. Uncles, aunts, cousins crowded around, drinking tea and smoking. This was back when one of them could send me to gas station to buy their cigarettes even though I was ten, and I got to keep the change. Later, a spare and sparse living room in Libby's and my first beat apartment, which sloped at an angle that could get a marble doing twenty miles per hour. Friends sat on all available seats; we had a wooden bowl with a cover that you could hit from and then toss to the next person. Many minor injuries occurred. Later, it would be art parties and gallery openings, days when we were hopelessly poor but we could show up and be fed, drink a bunch of wine, talk about high-end artistic ideas and visions of what art should be but hasn't been. Eventually, it was haughty lunches at the Harvard Club for the Manhattan Institute, chicken and rice and a nice desert, a guest speaker and everyone talking a little shop.

These kinds of gatherings, as it turns out, are not one of life's luxuries; they are a cornerstone of what it means to be human. Having never been denied that for months on end before, I had never really experienced what it means to get it back. It reminded me of my friend Alf who, some twenty-five years back, had gone to some remote part of Africa for some period of time in the Peace Corps. When he got back, he had a decidedly confused air about him, almost shocked by modernity; it was like he forgot how to sit on chairs.

After a few drinks, Sohrab relaxed and for a few hours, eventually on his building's roof with gleaming lights of midtown towers surrounding us, we almost played at normalcy. In a certain sense, the party was a first toe dipped into the water of going back to real life. This was happening all over America; it had occurred before the George Floyd protests with highly condemned pool parties and other gatherings gaining national attention and scolds, but after the protests started, it took on a new dimension. Although the protests and riots did not succeed in bringing the severe lockdowns to an end in places like New York City, they absolutely did embolden tons of people who had been on the stay-at-home fence to once more venture out.

As a personal example, the only reason that both Libby and I were able to attend Sohrab's soirée was that Charlie's friend's mom, who had been extremely cautious about getting the boys together, threw that caution to the wind and had the Captain stay over. This, again more for him than for us, was just another small piece of the puzzle that we hoped one day soon would show an image of life as we had previously known it.

But honestly, this turned out to be more than a social occasion. As is usual when a bunch of conservative journalists get together, talk soon tended toward work. In the previous year, Sohrab had emerged as a leading figure in a new kind of conservatism, one he would eventually and ironically call "woke conservatism." The primary way in which he did this was to set himself up against longtime *National Review* writer and constitutional lawyer David French in a rather aggressive screed attacking French.

The Ahmari versus French debate was inside baseball on the Right, but it was also extremely important. One of the frustrations for Trump-supporting conservatives, who were the vast, vast majority on the Right, was that throughout his presidency, the corporate media would feature "Never Trump" conservative voices as if they were somehow representative of some constituency of voters; they never really were. Either out of willful blindness or pure ignorance, "conservatives" like Bill Kristol, Max Boot, and Jennifer Rubin were presented as important voices on the Right, when by their own admission, they were barely even of the Right at all anymore.

Through happenstance, or maybe just a good sense of how to be at the right place at the right time, I found myself at an intersection of this new "woke" right. Sohrab was turning the *New York Post* opinion page into the flagship of this movement, but even before that, the *Federalist* had become a central outlet for this populist America-first and common-good conservatism. As the person who wrote most often for both, but who had been at first skeptical of some of Sohrab's radical ideas, I had a front-row seat to the fight, and if this had been an esoteric fight before the lockdowns, the five months of power-hungry state governments enacting crushing restrictions moved the arguments from the hypothetical to the very real.

At the heart of the initial Ahmari versus French debate was, of all things, a phenomenon known as Drag Queen Story Hour. Libraries were hosting events where sexually suggestive, mainly male to female, trans people read children stories to kids as young as toddlers. To Sohrab, as well as to almost everyone at the *Federalist*, this was an immoral situation that government had to put an end to. But for David French, the story hours were protected speech under the first amendment. He might not like it, or want his kids to go, but for us to restrict the progressives would open the door to progressives restricting all kinds of conservative and especially religious speech.

Coming from a basically classically liberal tradition of political thought, I was deeply sympathetic to French's arguments about maintaining constitutional norms. The extended lockdowns would change that, and not just for me. What became apparent was that French was offering a vision of a political transaction that progressives had no interest in honoring. The deal was basically we look the other way on Drag Queen Story Hour and the Left won't mess with things like church or freedom of political speech. For months, Americans had capriciously been denied their most basic constitutional rights, unless of course they were out on the streets protesting for progressive causes. The jig was up.

Furthermore, the new progressive religion was being given primacy; it received special dispensations. They were allowed to gather, they were allowed to, or at least were attempting to, as with the Seattle Police Department, hire and fire people based on race. The media, both traditional and social, were comfortable throttling the speech of conservatives to an extent that certain conversations were all but banned. The metaphysical idea that men can become women, for example, was simply no longer up for debate.

John Adams wrote that statesmen "may plan and speculate for Liberty, but it is Religion and Morality alone, which establish the Principles upon which Freedom can securely stand." That is to say that the constitution can and does establish a framework for freedom, but that it also leaves, by its very nature, much to the moral sensibilities of the citizenry. In the 1980s, Drag Queen Story Hour would not have been a thing, not because it the Constitution didn't protect it, but because it would have been deemed almost universally immoral. But now the religion of gender transubstantiation was not only deemed as equal to traditional religion, it was actually given primacy.

The Left had been actively trying to restrict religious expression for years, but when the lockdowns hit and the very act of going to church, even outside, even under the same conditions in which progressives gathered to worship at the altar of Marxism, was denied, then all of David French's fine ideas about rights and self-government seemed to melt under the heat of the hypocrisy.

The roots of Trumpian populism can be seen in the Reform Party of Ross Perot and Pat Buchanan's protectionist policies in the 1990s; its intellectual and political framework would be set in the work of writers like Michael Anton and Stephen Miller. But it was not until the lockdowns that less Trump-adjacent conservatives would come to the fore through Sohrab's Post opinion page, Tucker Carlson's wildly successful cable news show, and outlets like the *Federalist* that were up for a good fight. For all but a few on the Right, the suspension of so many rights for so long was a wake-up call that pushed away from Frenchism and into a more aggressive camp and posture. With or without Donald Trump, this is the new Right, and it will be for some time to come.

The idea that Republicans or conservatives were significantly divided in regard to Trump's response to the pandemic was simply never true. For every Republican governor like Larry Hogan of Maryland or Mike DeWine of Ohio who the media presented as deeply critical of Trump there were far more who approved of Trump's handling of the pandemic. For every Never Trumper who the corporate media paraded in front of its audiences to illuminate cracks on the Right, there were vastly more in Trump's corner.

Meanwhile, Democratic governors such as Steve Sisolak in Nevada and Jared Polis in Colorado had chosen far less restrictive measures than their party mates in New York and New Jersey, and yet the media never invented out of that some deep divide on the Left about how to respond to the virus. To pretend that only Trump sycophants agreed with his approach, the media needed "useful conservatives." But in reality, just as almost all conservatives and Republicans had come around to his presidency eventually, they also came around to his approach to Covid. And for all the mishaps and confusion on every level of government, there would be one shining example of success that Donald Trump deserves massive credit for. An accomplishment would occur that almost nobody thought possible, but the Trump administration made it happen anyway.

Chapter 13

◆

Myth 12—Trump Does Not Deserve Credit for Operation Warp Speed

I can be hapless at times. It was late July when I drove down to DC with Epstein, his bird, Uncle Rico, in a cage on my lap most of the way. I arrived a little late to the *Federalist* intern boot camp at our office in DC. For the first time since February, I left New York City. It wasn't until the next morning, when I was scheduled to interview head of Operation Warp Speed Dr. Moncef Slaoui, that I realized I had left my wallet in Brooklyn. I do this kind of thing too often, as you have seen. The first time I did *The McLaughlin Group* in DC, I left my suit pants in Brooklyn and had to do the show in jeans. This was extra embarrassing because the night before the filming, Meghan McCain had said to me, "You brought a suit, right?" To which I replied, "What am I, new?" Turns out, I brought half a suit.

The problem this time was that giant, important government office buildings like at Health and Human Services generally require identification that is a bit more robust than a Key Foods frequent shopper card, which is all I had other than a bank card. Thankfully, it was arranged that I would meet him in the lobby of the building after a temperature check. So at least I got to start things off looking like an idiot who forgets his driver's license.

It was about a week earlier when Americans began hearing about Operation Warp Speed. As I noted earlier in this book, work on a vaccine for the virus had begun almost before most Americans even knew there was a virus, back in January. But in May, Jared Kushner was tasked by the president with putting together a team that could deliver a vaccine, as well as therapeutic treatments as fast as possible. Hence reaching in the sci-fi nomenclature of *Star Trek* with "warp speed." Kushner assembled a team, led by Slaoui, and said "Engage."

The story of that name is somewhat amusing. On the day of the first press conference, the project was without a name. The communications team was somewhat at a loss, so they asked the scientists how they referred to it themselves. Sheepishly, the scientists said that they were *Star Trek* fans, so they called it Operation Warp Speed. The name stuck, and will no doubt go down in scientific history. Sometimes, that the way these things go.

At the beginning of the crisis, it was widely assumed that a vaccine was at least a year and a half away, putting its arrival somewhere in the late summer of 2021, and that wasn't even counting the efforts at production and distribution once a vaccine was found to be effective. That timeline led to a situation in which a vaccine was kind of an afterthought. After all, nobody really thought in March and April that severe restrictions would last a year and a half. The vaccine was something to be hopeful about, but not a quick cure for what ailed us. That was soon to change.

I had heard about Operation Warp Speed a few weeks earlier from my sources at HHS. At first, I couldn't get much on the record, so I didn't publicly write about it, though I was telling colleagues at the *Federalist* and elsewhere that what I was hearing was pretty positive stuff, that in fact a vaccine may well arrive long before anyone thought possible. When the White House finally started talking about it, I knew that I wanted to talk to Slaoui and get my own sense of just how confident he was in the potential of his team's efforts.

Dr. Slaoui is an elegant but somewhat severe man, even behind his powder-blue medical mask. I had never interviewed someone in a mask before. I was, of course, masked as well; it's not great. Not only was the recording on my phone muffled, but it was hard to create a rapport. There was one question I really wanted to ask him, but decided not to. In the days earlier, President Trump had begun touting Operation Warp Speed. As I said earlier, Operation Warp Speed had been in existence for some time but had not garnered much attention in the news media, which had labored since March under assumption that a vaccine was not possible until at least the summer of 2021.

The obvious question to ask now that several vaccines had moved miraculously into Phase 3 trials, the final step in the process, was whether one could be ready before the election. It was a tantalizing thought: Trump's ultimate October surprise, a vaccine as running mate that promised to end the nightmare of lockdown and death. But as much as I wanted to know, I did not want to fall into the trap I had so often criticized of politicizing what is really a public health issue, and I didn't want Slaoui to feel like this was an interview about politics—even though these days it seems everything is about politics.

So I asked him the more general question of whether a vaccine by the end of the year was a real possibility. Not only was it, he informed me, but it was very likely. The remarkable speed with which the vaccine had reached such a late stage of development was the result of almost limitless resources granted to the team assembled by Jared Kushner, who tapped Slaoui to lead it in mid-May. Part of the success they were achieving, he told me was ironically owing to the swift spread of the virus. Slaoui said he estimated at this point that between 15 and 25 percent of the American people had already contracted the virus, perhaps as high as 30 percent in hard-hit New York City. He also was extremely confident that the mortality rate for Covid-19 was between 0.3 and 0.5 percent. This echoed Trump's "hunch" from March, as well as Dr. Bhattacharya's seroprevalence study in April. The ability to have test subjects, of which thirty thousand needed to be recruited for each vaccine, in high-Covid areas meant that the results would be clearer and faster than would otherwise be possible.

He explained that the Coronavirus was unlike Ebola because it spread so fast but was not so deadly. Ebola killed upwards of 90 percent of its victims. He calmly told me that if there were ever a virus with the infection rate of Covid and the death rate of Ebola, it could be "a human extinction event." Scientists are weird, man. He didn't seem spooked by his statement at all; I, on the other hand, felt a kind of Edgar Allan Poe chill run down my spine.

The first vaccine that would prove to be successful came from Pfizer, just days after the November election. Unlike the Moderna effort, which had begun with federal government help in January, Pfizer had not taken any money from Operation Warp Speed for its research and development; it had, however, entered a distribution deal with the Trump administration worth billions of dollars.

So on November 9, when Pfizer announced that its Phase 3 trials had shown 90 percent efficacy for the vaccine, a number nobody had expected but would also be matched by Moderna a few days later, the first stories from the corporate media could not resist stating, wrongly, that Pfizer had not been a part of Operation Warp Speed. In fact, it was a spokesperson from Pfizer, no doubt wishing to distance the company from Trump, that originally told the *Times* they were not a part of Operation Warp Speed. They absolutely were. The company would walk back the statement later that day and confirm their participation.

One can understand, cowardly though it was, why Pfizer tried to distance itself from the administration. During the last few months of the election, time and again, Democrats including vice presidential candidate Kamala Harris and New York Gov. Andrew Cuomo had cast needless doubt on the vaccine process. Harris, for her part, made the rather bizarre claim that she would not trust a vaccine if Trump said it worked, as if somehow The Donald was in the lab with goggles on, mixing chemicals. Cuomo would go so far as to say that even if the FDA approved vaccines, he would have his own scientists review them before allowing New Yorkers to have it.

A strong case can be made that these doubts being expressed about the vaccines by Democrats represented the most irresponsible rhetoric of the entire pandemic response. By December, some polls would show that only 55 percent of Americans were willing to take a vaccine. Then President-Elect Joe Biden was asked if he would take the vaccine when approved, as former presidents Bill Clinton, George W Bush, and Barack Obama had promised to do. He answered that he would take it if Dr. Fauci said it was OK. But why? Dr. Fauci was a tireless public servant during the pandemic and certainly deserves the thanks of the American people for that, but he also got a lot wrong, whether it was mask wearing or schools, and after all, as Pete Rose once said of Nolan Ryan, "Dr. Fauci is Dr. Fauci but he's not God."

The clear indication from Biden here was that the FDA, and more broadly HHS, was not to be trusted because it was infected with Trumpism and the agencies might fudge things a bit to make the president look better, and this, mind you, was even after Biden had won the election. In fact, if anything, the opposite was true. Several people I spoke to in the administration spoke about what they called a resistance cell to the president, especially in the CDC. And one of the most notable examples of this resistance surrounded the promotion of the vaccines themselves.

The controversy started with a Politico story on September 29 citing numerous anonymous sources at HHS who objected to a series of public service announcements that the communications team at HHS had planned and had been allocated funds for in the late spring. The perfectly reasonable idea behind the campaign was to educate Americans about the vaccine and also to alleviate despair in a population that was growing ever wearier from lockdowns.

So what was the problem? A former Obama official laid it out in the Politico story. "CDC hasn't yet done an awareness campaign about Covid guidelines—but they are going to pay for a campaign about how to get rid of our despair? Run by political appointees in the press shop? Right before an election?" said Josh Peck, a former HHS official who oversaw the Obama administration's advertising campaign for HealthCare.gov. "It's like every red flag I could dream of."

Let's be perfectly clear: there was only ever one red flag and his name was Donald Trump. The concern of Peck and of the anonymous HHS officials was never that anything in the proposed ads was scientifically inaccurate or that bad information was being peddled, but rather that the lightning-fast movement on the vaccines could help Donald Trump politically. But the "controversy" was enough to scuttle the ad campaign. One PSA in particular that was never released but was desperately needed shows just how low the president's opponents were ready to go to defeat him.

Shulem Lemmer is not exactly a household name. But in the ultra-Orthodox Jewish communities of New York, he is a major celebrity. That community is famously insular, something along the lines of an urban Amish. Both city and state officials had struggled since the outset of the crisis to convince these traditional Jews in their black attire and tightly packed neighborhoods teeming with children to take the Covid restrictions seriously. The very good purpose behind the concept of the Lemmer PSA was to reach these people who do not engage in the mainstream cultural conversation with one of their own.

When turmoil hit, the program those in charge of it pushed for the Lemmer PSA to go forward even if the others would not because of the specific nature of the need, namely to get a message to people outside the traditional media infrastructure. According to multiple sources, they were told by higher-ups at that point that only PSAs for black and brown communities were under consideration any longer. A back-and-forth ensued in which the PSA was eventually filmed, but never released.

To put this in context, all of it happened at a time when officials in New York were struggling to stop outbreaks among the ultra-Orthodox. Their businesses, even their homes, were being raiding by authorities in a way that frankly no other community would see. This had been happening for months, in fact, with de Blasio shutting down Jewish funerals and even locking up playgrounds.

In October, Cuomo would say this about the controversial program targeting Jews:

"This is not a highly nuanced, sophisticated response. This is a fear-driven response, you know. This is not a policy being written by a scalpel; this is a policy being cut by a hatchet. It's just very blunt. I didn't propose this, you know; it was proposed by the Mayor [Bill de Blasio] in the City. I'm trying to sharpen it and make it better. But it's out of fear. People see the numbers going up—'Close everything! Close everything!' It's not the best way to do it, but it is a fear-driven response. The virus scares people. Hopefully, we get the numbers down in the zip codes, the anxiety comes down, and then we can have a smarter, more-tailored approach...the fear is too high to do anything other than, 'Let's do everything we can to get the infection rate down now, close the doors, close the windows.' That's where we are."

Cuomo's fear-driven response to the issues of the ultra-Orthodox communities might not have been needed had a serious outreach to those communities been made instead of the governor's petite pogroms. But that didn't happen, and it didn't happen specifically because officials at HHS did not want to help Trump. So to argue that HHS was going to be less than honest about vaccines in an effort to support Trump simply makes no sense. By the fall, Big Pharma was running public service ads very similar in concept to those proposed by HHS in the summer.

There is simply no way to look at what Operation Warp Speed accomplished without acknowledging it as a tremendous triumph for Trump and his administration. And it was achieved at considerable risk. By deciding to enter production on vaccines before they were even approved, we had millions of doses by the end of the year. But had the trials failed, we would have wasted millions of dollars. This was a very Trumpy risk to take. In addition, HHS cut considerable red tape. It may well be that in the single term of a Trump presidency with many accomplishments, none were more important than vaccine development. Not just for America, but for the world. And not just in terms of this specific pandemic, but in terms of how we handle future viruses.

Trump would not quite get his October surprise of a vaccine running mate, but he would come very close. The Democrats and the media would continue to heap doubt on the effort until they were secure in a Biden victory, and even after that, most would roundly refuse to give Trump credit.

And then something even worse happened. Some officials and pundits on the Left began suggesting that even with the vaccines, our lives would not fully come back to normal. That precautions such as masks and social distancing would continue well past the level of vaccination needed to protect the population.

This was a question I had specifically asked Slaoui in July. Being a former theater guy, I put it in the context of a Broadway show. The Great White Way had gone dark in March; once enough people were immunized, I asked Slaoui, would people be able to attend a packed Broadway show without wearing a mask? He didn't hesitate; he assured me that they would be able to. Yet once the vaccine started to become available, other experts were saying the opposite. Dr. Fauci himself would vacillate wildly on how much of the population needed to be vaccinated. He then incredibly told the *New York Times* in December that he based his estimates on public polling, edging the number up as he saw the numbers willing to be vaccinated increase. It gave the game away. Fauci was not giving us unvarnished facts and letting the body politic come to judgments. He was doling out information in an effort to manipulate, not to inform. He was treating the American people like children. It wasn't about science. It was about power.

Chapter 14

───◆───

Myth 13—Nobody Likes Lockdowns

As devastating as the lockdowns had been to industries like restaurants, hospitality, travel, and retail, there were, of course, also economic winners. The most significant winners tended to be in the tech sector. Whether it was the wildly enhanced need for video conferencing and other modes of communication or delivery of food and supplies from companies like Amazon, the atomized new normal was a massive boon for them.

Among the industries that got that boon out of the Coronavirus lockdown were adult entertainment and sex work. This makes a lot of sense if you think about it; people were stuck at home with little but internet access, they weren't going out on dates, and many needed something that felt like a total escape much more than usual, which also helps to explain the uptick in drug and alcohol use. Pornhub, the most famous mostly free porn site in the country, saw as much as a 20 percent uptick in use by May. This was a different kind

DIY craze, but I'm not knocking it; as Woody Allen once said, "It's sex with someone you love."

The traditional porn and strip club industries were in some ways the hardest hit by the lockdown. Porn studios that do high-end production were closed down just like any other movie or TV studio, and strip clubs, while they remained open in some places, were closed in most. In a lot of ways, though, those institutions were already losing their dominance in the area of sex work. Just as the videotape cassette player was the dawn of the doom of the pornographic movie theater, so did the internet, and especially the rise of high-quality streaming, usher in new ways of doing the world's oldest work.

Amid this phenomenon, the website OnlyFans took center stage, not only as a place for those seeking pleasures of their own flesh, but for those who are willing to provide the service. Interactive one-on-one video porn had long been a subgenre of the industry, kind of like Zoom but with nudity and fetishes. Sites like Chaturbate offer public feeds, which is to say anyone and multiple people can watch at once with the option to go private for an added fee.

Although there are certainly strong moral arguments to be made against porn, even before the pandemic, it was becoming a much more normalized part of Americans' lives. Even the *Federalist*, an outlet with some libertarian roots, but at this point more connected to the woke social conservativism of Ahmari and Carlson, published a post by the porn star Brandi Love decrying those very social conservatives' concerns about porn.

Love was responding to an opinion piece by Charlie Peters in the *American Conservative* in which he, I imagine jokingly, said that the rise of porn, and especially sites like OnlyFans, made him wonder if living under a global Islamic caliphate might be a better fate. Love, the rare conservative in the adult industry, took issue, writing, "In contrast to the absurd idea that living under the draconian restrictions of Sharia law would be better than the freedom for people to do things you think are wrong, let's look at how adult entertainment is not only legally protected but also providing relief during the current pandemic."

Regardless of where one stands on the issue of the morality of this particular form of "relief," there was evidence to suggest that many Americans were finding solace in their atomized evenings of internet-connected self-pleasure. After all, if groceries and electronics could be ordered online and left on your stoop without any actual human contact, then why could not sexual gratification also be provided without the danger of disease, sexual or otherwise. And for some, perhaps very lonely men, this may well have been a needed if not entirely healthy form of connection.

I spoke with Las Vegas-based sex worker Empress Daisy Delfino (Known as Empress Delfina) about the impact of the lockdown on her industry and how it colored and shaded the work that she does. Delfino is a twenty-four-year veteran of the industry who had for many years even prior to the lockdown embraced the opportunities that faster digital internet speeds provide her. She has regular clients with whom she crafts the sexual aspect of the interactive experience. Obviously, there is no touching or penetrative sex, but the emotional aspect of sex is apparently quite present.

I asked Empress Delfina, which is her "stage" name and Twitter handle, if she also experienced the uptick in business described by the numbers in the rest of the industry, and to her surprise, she did. "I thought people would not want to spend out of fear," she told me, but the exact opposite happened. Though she wasn't trying to aggressively promote or market herself during this time, she did pick up a few new clients. "They found me," she said. But most of the uptick was regulars using her service more. This was, for many industries, one of the interesting twists of the lockdown; people couldn't go out to eat, or to the movies, or to a sporting event, so even if they saw their income reduced, they often still wound up with a certain level of disposable income and limited ways to spend it.

I was curious if the pandemic itself came up during her time with her clients, and was surprised by her emphatic, "Oh yes!" I think I was surprised because I had assumed that since this was an escape from the lockdown, it would not be front and center within the interactive experience. But what I failed to take into account, and what I think many people fail to take into account about sex work, is the emotional bond and support that the mostly men who engage in it (on the consumer side) find from the objects of their sexual desire.

According to Delfino, not only did the lockdown come up often, the men were expressing fear to her about it. Perhaps either with few other outlets with whom to express their emotions, or from a hesitation that those in their "real lives" would view them as weak, they were able to express themselves much the way one might to a therapist while, obviously doing stuff you can't really do with a therapist, even if you're Jeffrey Toobin. This aspect of sex work is not entirely new. Even strippers in traditional clubs will try to create emotional connections with the clientele, as Shakespeare put it, "Therefore I lie with her and she with me/And in our faults by lies we flatter'd be." But one can readily imagine the privacy and safety of the online-only experience enhancing, not reducing, that emotional aspect of the work.

One client that Delfino described to me did indeed start spending way more time with her, and money on doing so, up until the time when he was laid off. She continued to provide emotional support. "I wasn't just going to drop him completely because he couldn't buy my content," she told me, but I gathered the purely sexual element was either seriously curtailed or gone. She was worried about him, told him to feel free to reach out, and was concerned enough that she gave him the suicide prevention hotline number should he need it.

The Empress told me that as the clubs started shutting down, and even in some cases without them shutting down, but with dancers quite reasonably scared to perform, many performers turned to online work. For her, this was a blessing. As she put it, it made people who had once been uninterested in sex workers suddenly "less whore-aphobic." "Even the bottle service girls were turning to sex work," she told me. As were thousands of women across the country, whether they were out of work or just curious about this business.

Not everyone was as thrilled as the Empress by these developments, however. For social conservatives and some others wary of the effects of pornography on our society, the lockdown made their work of dissuading people from engaging in being a sex work customer that much harder. They want, if not whore-aphobia, at least a healthy understanding of the possibilities of addiction and what they argue becomes a barrier to actual real-life intimacy when the expectations of sex can be controlled by a credit card.

As it turned out, I maintained some communication with Empress Delfina after our interview—no, not that kind. We chatted on Twitter, mostly about the election; she is, shall we say, not a fan of Donald Trump. And she took a curious, unorthodox approach to helping Joe Biden's chances at election. She began a new phone sex service, which she called "Trump Conversion Therapy." Callers who supported Trump would be berated by her, presumably after being informed what she was wearing, and made to chant things like "I am Putin's Puppet."

As Election Day neared, Delfina claimed on Twitter that she was advising these clients of hers to make penance for their Trump support by—how shall I say this?—um, putting a certain object into a certain orifice when they went to the polls. Whatever floats your boat, I guess. I don't think she swayed the election, although she did claim to have a lot of "Johns," or should it be "Donalds," in swing state Pennsylvania, but hey, points for creativity.

But of course, it was not only porn and sex work that got an economic boost from the lockdowns; almost every industry that relies heavily on the internet did incredibly well owing to the swell in demand. It was always the goal of Big Tech to move shoppers away from brick-and-mortar stores and toward shopping online; this shift was well underway before the pandemic. But it is difficult to imagine a scenario more beneficial to the tech industry than people literally being told not to leave their houses. And given the fact that the tech sector now also provides a huge percentage of Americans with their news and information, this created a serious and dangerous conflict of interest.

Companies like Google, Facebook, and Twitter controlled and often times censored what information about the pandemic and lockdown we could see. This could be viewed as erring on the side of caution, but it was clearly also in their economic interests and in the interest of the entire tech sector. One does not need to imagine some vast conspiracy theory to understand that Big Tech was in a serendipitous situation in which the responsible actions of censorship and manipulation of information to save lives were also making them an enormous amount of money. And that money was coming at the expense of sectors like dining and retail.

At the beginning of the lockdowns in March, we saw advertisers reacting with messages of general support, and as Jim O'Neil told me, this really was organic and a matter of quickly responding to trends. There was no time for strategy. But as more months were torn from the calendar, the ads started to change. Now the tech companies that were reaping record profits were also patting themselves on the back for saving people's lives. Big Tech has always had a savior complex, a desire to save the world, as it were, and now it could happily present itself as a force for good, protecting the population from a deadly disease. But there is a bit of a chicken-and-egg question at work here.

There is little doubt that twenty-five years ago, with the state of the internet and its adjacent technologies much more primitive, the kind of lockdowns we had in 2020 would have been simply impossible. Millions of workers could not have telecommuted to work; the widespread distribution of goods and services could not have been managed logistically online, and certainly, there could be no remote learning for our children. The point here is that although it true that Big Tech made our lives easier in the pandemic, it also made many aspects of the lockdowns possible.

In July of 2019, Libby had written a piece for the British publication *UnHerd* about the rise of machines in our lives. She based the piece on the 1909 E. M. Forster story 'The Machine Stops." She described it this way, "The eerily prescient tale opens with Vashti, a woman who doesn't leave her underground home. She doesn't need to. No one leaves their little cells to venture out in to a post-apocalyptic world. They don't have to: all needs are met by an omnipotent 'Machine'. Communication with others is done via instant messaging and video conferencing. In any case, people have no inclination to meet up; they only want to share ideas. And the Machine knows what you want, without you having to ask…"

Eerily prescient indeed. Long before *Ready Player One*, Forster had already envisioned a virtual world in which human contact was obsolete. And it was not a cheery tale; it was a warning about the possibility of machines destroying the fundamental fabric of what being a human is. Whether Big Tech is actively trying to take advantage of the Covid crisis to produce this more atomized society or not, it is being created and they are the primary beneficiaries. This is something we must keep very much in mind when as a society we consider how to combat this kind of pandemic.

It was only a year after Forster wrote "The Machine Stops" that in 1910, the Irish writer George William Russell, better known as Æ, would coin the phrase "Experts ought to be on tap, and not on top," that Glenn Loury referenced to me. It's worth looking at the context of the quote from his article in the *Irish Homestead*:

"Our theory, which we have often put forward, is that **experts ought to be on tap and not on top.** We have had during our career a long and intimate knowledge of experts, most interesting men in their own speciality to which they have devoted themselves with great industry and zeal. But outside this special knowledge they are generally as foolish and ignorant as any person one could pick up in the street, with no broad knowledge of society or the general principles of legislation."

What we see here is that over a century ago, our culture's great thinkers were already tackling the very specific issues that we faced with the virus. And more than anything, what they were saying was to push back against technology and expertise. Why? Because free people need to have a say in how their society functions. And our traditional freedoms and way of life are under direct attack from the forces of technology and expertise, in fact it's even hidden. In his book *Apollo's Arrow: The Profound and Enduring Impact of Coronavirus on the Way We Live*, Nicholas Christakis all but assures us that our lives will never be the same again, and that we must trust in our experts and elites.

In fact, this was Christakis's position all along. As early as March 9, he composed a Twitter thread that would basically wind up in his book in which he widely praised the Chinese response to the virus and urged America to adopt much of it. Just like McKinsey, he saw a great opportunity to bring the population of the United States to heel. As with so much of the response to the virus, it was much more about power than it was about science. As the months dragged on, the political and economic forces that benefitted from the lockdowns found greater resolve to pronounce that we would never go back to normal.

So when we hear from the proponents of lockdowns that nobody likes it, nobody wants it, and everybody hates it, we should take that with a grain of salt. There are very powerful forces in the world that like this situation just fine. They aren't quite willing to admit that in most cases yet, but they are certainly getting there. We have to ask ourselves the question: in one hundred years, do we want the United States to be more like China or do we want China to be more like the United States? Millions of immigrants who flee Communist China, flocking to the free shores of America, have one answer, but Big Tech and its allies in politics may well have a very different one.

Chapter 15

Myth 14—We Must Remain in Doom and Gloom

On the evening of Thursday, October 1, I was scheduled to appear on Laura Ingraham's show on Fox News. I love doing Laura's show; she's very funny and clever, but it also appears in the 10 p.m. hour, which frankly is a little late for me. I'm a morning guy in general, up by 5:30, writing by 6. So looking awake and nicely dressed at 10:30 at night is a struggle.

This was the main reason I called Libby to see if she Charlie wanted to go out to dinner. I could kill like two hours and by the time I got home, it would already be around 8:30. We went to a little pub called Skinflints in Bay Ridge, and as it turned it out, we dined inside in New York City for the first time since March. We had to get a temperature check and fill out our contact information, but after that, we were eating in a restaurant, almost like normal. After the meal, we had to put our masks on for the short walk to the door. Charlie quipped,

"Right, because sitting down is a Coronavirus blocker." Skepticism had reached the preteen set.

After dinner, it was back to my place, where a studio van would be waiting for me. Another strange wrinkle of the virus. All television, even the news, is a matter of both style and substance. This was exacerbated by the pandemic and lockdown in a way that was quite simply unprecedented. The big three cable news networks, CNN, Fox News, and MSNBC, have always looked—at least in terms of their sets— pretty similar. Big desks, fancy well-lit backdrops; nobody wants their show to look like a schlub until and unless they do. When the shutdowns hit New York and Washington, DC, where most of the national cable news coverage is shot, the studios more or less closed. Just as in our private and business lives, we started seeing guests on cable news shows from their own homes on not-so-great laptop cameras.

It served as yet another mental reminder, as if we needed any more, that we were not living in normal times. The ugly and abnormal look of the news was literally a part of the story they were covering. When CNN anchor Chris Cuomo came down with the virus, doing his show from his basement where he was, or so he claimed, imprisoned, it became a huge part of his coverage. That was true even up to the point when he finally emerged to his waiting family, the moment he had waited two weeks for. We eventually found out that was all staged nonsense, but the point is that the producers at CNN knew exactly what they were doing, what message they were trying to send.

In some ways, MSNBC was even worse. It often seem like they were literally asking their guests to use the worst lighting possible and present a general look of being bedraggled. What you see is, as they say, what you get and to show a shiny, good-looking news product would undermine the general attitude of lockdown sadness they were eager to instill in the public.

Fox News was an exception, especially the primetime shows. When I did Carlson's show on May 21, the producer called me and asked if there was a good place for the van to park near my apartment in Brooklyn. He explained that in lieu of a studio, the network had been using vans fitted out with cameras, lighting, and backdrops. The idea behind this was to present as normal-looking a product as possible for viewers. The vans were not exclusive to Fox; other networks also used them, but Fox's producers in particular wanted a normal look. In early September, with the studios still closed, journalist Chadwick Moore was given a car to my place so we could both use the van, him in the top and me in the bottom of the hour.

I have to say they are super cool vehicles and really do present a look that is almost indistinguishable from a studio. The first time I used one, Charlie who wants to be a YouTube star, came out to see it and get a little tour from the operator who also drives it. He stared, wide-eyed, covetous even, and just said, "Nice." This is very high praise from my ten-year-old son.

There was only one glitch, really, aside from the fact that in the summer months it was hot as hell and the air conditioning couldn't be used because it would be picked up by the mics, and that was a slight sound delay. Some of you who are devotees of primetime cable news may have noticed that at the top of most interviews, the "thanks for being with us" opening would get a bit wonky, with host and guest briefly talking over each other. Eventually, I stopped saying anything when greeted and just gave a little smile. That seemed to work.

Eventually, I kind of got a regular van guy. Late twenties, I think, a painter who lives in my old stomping ground, the Lower East Side. Man. To be that age and in New York, the whole city, the whole universe in front of you. Terrifying beauty of hope and danger. I told him stories of Williamsburg in the late '90s, when I was pretty much him. That's what you do. That's the New York generational transaction. And he wanted to know it. Just like I wanted to know about Warhol's

East Village when I was being told stories of Gotham. It's all a cycle, a widening gyre. Anyway, I like the kid.

Checking my phone just before the hit, I saw that White House aide Hope Hicks had contracted the Coronavirus. I think it was Bedford who said something like "what if Trump gets it?" via email. I did my hit about Andrew Cuomo's dictatorial powers and settled back in the living room to wind down. Doing primetime hits is a bit like doing a theater show: it amps you up, at least it amps me up, and it's hard to just tuck into bed right after. So I was up when the news hit the wire about 1 a.m. Trump had Covid. I rolled an unusually large joint and slowly smoked, TV on mute, images of the White House and president slowly blurring as my mind wandered at all the possible outcomes. Only one seemed certain. The next day was going to be incredibly stupid.

Upon waking up, the parade of absurd takes was already marching merrily through social media like the final scene in *The Music Man*, and just like those seventy-six trombones, this concert was also pretend. First, we had "Does he really have it?" This was couched as a question, of course: "How can we believe that he really has it given all the lies this administration tells?" Then we moved into "The doctors are lying about how serious it is." This was followed by "Who has he infected? Why does he hate masks?"

After spending the morning continuously smacking the top of my head to knock my eyeballs out of a permanent rolled position, I started to see the media narrative crystalize. This was a Greek tragedy. Trump was being punished for his hubris, falling victim to his own devices; the milquetoast moderate line became "We wish the president well, but why did he allow this to happen?"

While the president was at Walter Reed, something truly despicable happened, but something pretty wonderful happened, too. The former was a ridiculous smearing of the doctors at Walter Reed by the news media, which relentlessly insisted each day that the American people were not being given the full story. Was the president on oxygen? They breathlessly demanded to know. What drugs was he on? This was simply another example of a deranged media that had long since decided that any information coming from Trump's orbit must be assumed to be false, a lie, or at best, carefully chosen words to stroke the president's ego. This was just like months earlier, when Dr. Fauci had been asked if his statements about the virus were voluntary, to which he rightfully took offense. It was an unhinged attempt by the media to sow doubt in the American people where none was warranted.

When Chief of Staff Mark Meadows said a day into Trump's illness that "He had a very concerning night," the mantra of trust the science went out the window. Even though the president's doctors were saying that he was recovering, surely Meadows had accidently given away the truth that Trump was at death's door. After all, no official statements were ever to be believed; the truth had to pilfered from accidental admissions.

Then on Sunday, three days into his diagnosis, Trump absolutely broke the media by, of all things, taking a drive around the block. No sooner had the president been admitted to Walter Reed than supporters began showing up with Trump flags outside the facility to wish him well. The first few were scurried away, but by the next day, a solid crowd was there sending their love and best wishes.

If there is anything that Donald Trump loves, it is a large crowd of his supporters, so he made a decision to leave his presidential suite at Walter Reed and drive around the block to acknowledge those who had come out for him. Obviously, as any idiot would know, this was cleared by the doctors and measures were taken to protect to the driver of the limo and the Secret Service officer protecting Trump. A Plexiglas partition separated Trump in the backseat, and everyone in the vehicle was masked.

This, of course, did not stop a complete media freak-out over the incident. How dare Trump put the lives of the others with him in danger, never mind that the Secret Service officer is with Trump almost constantly? What a terrible example to send to the American people, selfish, callous, arrogant. It all rained down. One physician from Walter Reed, not one who was treating the president, of course, decried the incident. "Every single person in the vehicle during that completely unnecessary Presidential 'drive-by' just now has to be quarantined for 14 days. They might get sick. They may die. For political theater. Commanded by Trump to put their lives at risk for theater. This is insanity," Dr. James Phillips tweeted.

Before I go any further, it might be useful to point out, in narrator voice, "Nobody died."

It would be a weekend that proved a microcosm of the entire Coronavirus crisis, down to the detail. It moved from utter hysteria that Trump would die or suffer greatly, to resignation that maybe the situation wasn't that dire, but still, he's irresponsible for not taking more preventative measures, to him being more or less fine and going so far as leaving Walter Reed hospital to tell Americans not to live in fear of the virus. But of course, nobody knew that would be the result on Friday morning, just as nobody knew much back in March.

The diagnosis and the confusion surrounding it would wreak havoc on the election; the second debate would eventually be cancelled outright, in part through Trump's kneejerk reaction to reject a virtual debate. In the end, everyone in the president's circle who contracted the virus turned out to be fine. The infections appeared to stem from the Rose Garden reception announcing Amy Coney Barrett as Trump's nominee to replace the recently deceased Supreme Court Justice Ruth Bader Ginsburg. It was, or so said the media, a superspreader event. A few hundred people gathered, very few masks, some hugging and glad-handing,

I watched the event from a small airport outside Harrisburg, where the president was holding a rally that night. That was an event with several thousand people, and also very few masks, this created an interesting dichotomy between the events. At the White House, testing for the virus was de rigueur; even people who were essentially asymptomatic were found positive, such as Trump's son Barron. Did the virus spread at the Harrisburg rally as well? Probably? Trump did over a dozen of these outdoor airport rallies, and yet none of them led to any detectable major outbreak, and trust me, had that happened the news media would have made damn sure that we knew about it.

On November 3, 2020 I drank a coffee and had a few smokes on the front porch before walking around the corner to my polling place. For weeks, I had seen video of people standing in massive lines waiting to vote; I was pretty sure I wouldn't suffer that fate. In my whole twenty-plus years of voting, I don't think I've ever waited more than ten minutes to vote. I'm not sure I can explain why that is, but it held form. As a New Yorker, my vote for president was utterly meaningless, but there was a competitive House race between Democratic incumbent Max Rose and GOP challenger Nicole Malliotakis that I was excited to have my small democratic say in. Bubbles inked and ballot slipped into the machine, my civic duty was done and it was off to Penn Station, off to Washington, DC.

Most of the stores on 34th Street were boarded up. This wasn't entirely new; it had been the case in the summer at the peak of the looting in NYC, but now it was back. I would see the same thing in Washington later that day, and in Philly the day after the election. The reason for this, as best as I could tell, was a fear that should Trump win, there would be riots and looting. But just as there was no way to deny that the lockdowns and the listless boredom they engendered had encouraged the summer of rage, the boarded windows were just another piece of the transformed plastic of urban reality.

One had to struggle to remember what these cities had looked like just a year earlier. Now, outdoor seating at eateries poured into half the street; many of the businesses not boarded up were simply abandoned. Those who were out on the street were mainly masked, leaving little but staring eyes atop the bodies wandering about. That these changes were wrought in a mere nine months should have been shocking, but so slow had those months seemed, more standstill than passage of time, that much to my chagrin, it almost felt normal to me. Almost.

There was a general sense among people that after the election, regardless of the winner, the nature of the pandemic and the response to it would change. This was more vocalized by those on the Right who believed that most of the media had been stoking fear to hurt President politically, but even on the Left, one could sense that one way or the other, the temperature of pandemic panic was set to go down. After all, vaccines were on their way. Aside from the first two or three weeks of relative bipartisanship in the face of the virus, the election and the pandemic were of apiece, each having its impact on the other. When I started working on this book in June, the election seemed like a side story. As the train whipped me down to the nation's capital, it was clear that the two had been inexorably intertwined.

The week before, I had been in Pennsylvania with Bedford, reporting from some swing counties there. It was hard to fathom that back in February, he and I had been in New Hampshire, unaware what was about to befall the nation. But there we were. I had sat down with Lee Snover, the GOP committee chairwoman for Northampton County, to get a feel for where things stood. Her biggest fear was that suburban women, who she said had "lost their minds over Covid," were fleeing Trump. I was a bit dubious; after all, these voters had shifted in the 2018 midterms as well, but she was talking about more than politics. She was talking about her own personal experiences, her friends and family. She had lost her father to Covid, but told me defiantly that she had no fear of it.

I had no idea what was going to happen on Election Day. I thought it would be closer than expected, but beyond that, it seemed like a crapshoot. I thought Trump would win Pennsylvania, and said so on Laura Ingraham's show a few nights earlier. As it turned out, Mollie Hemingway was on right after my segment. She heard me predict that the Keystone State would stay red. A few minutes later, I got an email to one of our *Federalist* lists, "WTF Marcus..." it read. I have a reputation at the outlet for bad predictions, and in retrospect, should have been more circumspect.

Throughout election night, we did a livestream video from the office, Bedford, Ben, Emily Jashinsky, and I breaking down results as they came in. To say the early results for Trump were promising would be an understatement. Once it was clear he won Florida, we knew this would not be a blowout. As more and more results came in, it looked very good for Trump; the betting line moved dramatically to favoring a Trump victory. On a radio hit I did at about 10 p.m., host Dan Proft seemed convinced that Trump had done it and was speaking in those terms. I wasn't so sure; maybe it's because I'm a Philly sports fan, but I knew that leads were finicky and often erased. Still, when I climbed into bed at 2:30 a.m. after Trump's remarks, I thought things looked good for him.

"In the morning it was morning and I was still alive." That Charles Bukowski quote was the first line in my *New York Post* column Wednesday morning. Sohrab had asked me to write the conciliatory, "we are all Americans no matter who wins" piece. He wanted it grand and writerly, easy enough. And, hell, like everything else I write, I believed it. Now I was drinking coffee and smoking on the back porch of the *Federalist* office, and things seemed murkier than the night before. I needed a break, so I Ubered to Georgetown to have breakfast with my friend and art critic Billy Newton. Under the November sun of a breezy cool alleyway, we ate eggs and talked about paintings and beauty. I needed that.

Back at the office, it was becoming clear that the Coronavirus had one more trick to play on the election. We had known for weeks, maybe even months, that with so many states changing their election laws to keep people out of polling places, a tactic that, in retrospect, was probably not needed, tallying results would be a strange new experience. Many people predicted that it would take a week if not longer to know for sure who won; as it turned out, that was pretty much right. Throughout the day, strong Trump leads were shrinking; mail-in ballots that had been piling up since September were opened, and like a ghostly echo from the near past, they were breaking heavily to Joe Biden.

Two questions began to emerge as all of this was going on. First, given that Trump had been nipping at Biden's lead for a good two or three weeks going into the election, had the record-breaking early mail-in voting hurt his chances? Second, and more sinister, was the possibility that all of this newfangled voting occasioned by the virus had made fraud easier to pull off. The president had been alleging this for months, and not entirely without cause. Attorney General Bill Barr had warned that these voting methods were more open to tampering, but in general, the media had dismissed this idea as paranoid politicking.

In my Uber back to the office, I had somewhere in the neighborhood of a billon texts and emails that had gone unchecked as Billy and I discussed the complicated legacy of Clement Greenberg. The most urgent of these was from Bedford, informing me that we were going to Philly that afternoon to investigate voter fraud. I was dubious and a little frustrated. Even though I fundamentally agreed with Trump that having so much mail-in voting was a bad idea, even that it invited fraud, it seemed entirely implausible to me that enough could be proven to change whatever the result was going to be. On the other hand, there would be soft pretzels.

Sure enough, we did get reports of election abuses, mostly off the record. Republican observers had been denied access to polling and counting stations; there were allegations of ballot stuffing. Now, I mean, all of that is bad, of course, but I grew up in Philly, following its politics pretty closely. We used to say that if a local politician didn't get indicted at least once, he wasn't working hard enough. I was exhausted and this errand felt pointless. Not only that, by the evening of the fourth, things had seemingly swung in Biden's direction for good.

It would be three more days until the networks were ready to call the race. Saturday, in the 11 a.m. hour, it happened. Joe Biden was president-elect. The masked basement cowboy had pulled it off. But not by much: this was not a drastic repudiation of Trump, or his response to the pandemic. Once again, massive crowds took to the streets in New York, DC, and Philly. Mayor Bill de Blasio, who had been hassling Orthodox Jews for having outdoor gatherings in the low hundreds in what Cuomo had called a fear tactic, came out to Brooklyn to celebrate with the massive crowds. In Manhattan, Sen. Chuck Schumer, at times sans mask, partied with the people.

By now, the hypocrisy of it all had lost some of its sting but none of its irony. This time, there wasn't even the absurd excuse that the crowds were fighting the public health crisis of racism. The only thing progressives and Democrats could really say was that at least they were wearing masks. I think most people saying this knew how half-assed it was; after all, if this was fine, why not outdoor concerts with masks? Why not baseball games? Why not Jewish funerals? They had no answer this time. But with the election all but over, they really didn't need one. That night, Notre Dame would beat number-one Clemson in double overtime; as the final play ended, students rushed the field by the thousands. Once again, many people asked themselves, "Is it over now?"

The Covid election of 2020 was a loss for Trump, but he did not lose with Republicans as many hoped he would; there was no GOP revolt against the president. He lost by about the same margins in critical states as he had won with four years earlier. Republicans made solid gains in the House of Representatives, and seemed poised to hold the Senate pending runoff elections in Georgia. With the possible exception of the economy, with which it was closely linked, no issue had been more important to the election than the Coronavirus. But for all of the efforts of Democrats and their media allies to paint Trump's response as an utter disaster, the voters didn't seem to buy it. Cases in Europe, presumably not

Trump's fault, were spiking those nations into further lockdowns. It may well be true that without the lockdowns, Trump might have won, but it seemed to cost him only on the margins politically.

Ben had sent an email a few days earlier highlighting a March 30 report from NBC News in which Dr. Deborah Birx had said that the US would have up to two hundred thousand deaths "if we do things almost perfectly." Clearly, we had not done things almost perfectly, and the numbers of deaths reflected that, reaching over three hundred thousand by the year's end. There were debates about what actually constitutes a Covid death; did everyone who died with Covid die from Covid? Progressive media types like Chris Hayes would blather on Twitter about how Trump had killed hundreds of thousands, but it was absurd. Not just because as Birx had said in March, there was always going to be significant death, but because nobody had or has ever pointed to any series of actions taken by Trump and shown that had he acted otherwise, significant numbers of deaths would have been avoided.

With Trump, there was never that smoking gun as there was with Cuomo and the nursing homes; there was never that moment or decision where had he gone another way, the virus would have been much better contained. We know this is true because had there been one, it would have been at the center of Biden's campaign. It wasn't because it doesn't exist. The hard to explain and painful truth displayed more or less around the world was that you cannot hide from a virus. You can mitigate it, and we did, but mitigation is porous, and at a certain point, the diminishing returns of shutting everything down cause their own suffering and death.

By the time I dragged my weary self back to Brooklyn, I could also sense in some kind of new way that personally, things were starting to open up and lighten. Charlie had been in a learning pod at his music school for two months and Libby was now of the opinion that he should switch into a blended learning model that would have him in his real school two days a week. He was relieved and very happy at the change as there had been only girls at the pod and now he would see his guy friends again.

The slow New York City opening had finally started to feel something closer to normal, at least in some ways. David Bernstein, who throws happy hours for New York conservative types, announced that on November 11 the first event since February would occur, at a bar. The week before, I had rushed home from Pennsylvania to pick up Charlie so that Libby could get to a theater performance in the Village; it was outdoors, but at least it was theater.

The Friday night after the election, I ventured to a local bar that I noticed was open again. Aside from there being no stools at the bar, it was almost normal. I met some people, including a guy I'm pretty sure is in the Mob. Among other thing, when I bought him a drink and said, "Here you go, my friend," he said, "I'm not your friend," but not in a menacing way. Friend has a special meaning in La Cosa Nostra, as fans of the movie *Donnie Brasco* will know. The place had to close at 11, but I wound up with him in his car with two women I didn't know headed to a bar in Sunset Park with the iron shutter half-closed. Inside, there was music and booze and barstools and even smoking. Dare I say, a flowering return of civilization?

Experts were still warning about things like large Thanksgiving gatherings California governor Newsom announcing absurd and unenforceable restrictions on things like singing in your own house, but you could sense that for many people, even those who just a month or two earlier were dubious about gathering indoors, a tide was changing. But not everywhere and not equally. In December, Gov. Cuomo would suspend indoor dining in New York City, even though his own contact tracing data showed that restaurants accounted for just 1.4 percent of the viral spread. In California, Gov. Newsom was issuing stay-at-home orders, but despite his rigorous approach to lockdown, the virus stormed back in the Golden State.

Meanwhile, Florida and Texas were more or less open. And New Yorkers and Californians were voting by moving truck what approach they liked better. New York State lost over one hundred twenty-six thousand residents between July 2019 and July 2020, and that only covers the first four months of the lockdowns. Now these trends had existed before the pandemic, the New York to Miami or Los Angeles to Austin move, but the pandemic exacerbated the phenomenon. Many of our cities that locked down most dramatically suffered such devastating economic loss that true recovery may well be a generational project. Meanwhile, the states that stayed more open have a much clearer path to economic recovery and growth.

It comes back to the idea that the tie goes to the runner. No reasonable case can be made that the states that chose the strongest lockdowns achieved significantly better Covid outcomes. That is the bottom line. That is why this must never happen again.

Conclusion

America Must Choose Freedom

In high school, I had a history and politics teacher named Pat Reifsnyder. Pat was a bit of a legend at Germantown Friends School by the time I took a class with her. We butted heads quite a bit, but I learned a lot from Reify about the duplicity of ward leaders, of which she was one, about not pulling a straight ticket, about reading local politics in the *Philadelphia Inquirer* each morning. But she had a quirk I recall, as well. She really hated the expression "live free or die."

Her aversion to the old revolutionary saw makes sense given that it was a Quaker school, nonviolence and all that, but mainly, she viewed it as a false choice. And in the early 1990s, in fact, for most of my life, it seemed that way. A choice between liberty and death felt like something in a history book, not a living, breathing maxim. The pandemic and the lockdowns that ensued created a new maxim though: "live free *and* die" or even "live free and you are killing people." In a way not seen in living memory, the protection of basic constitutional rights and the protection of human life

259

were, at least it was argued by many, at fundamental odds with each other.

Before digging too deeply into the battle between rights and public health, it is important to remember that the founding generation, the one that enumerated the rights granted to us by God and nature, was very well aware of pandemics and the havoc and death associated with them. Dolley Madison's first husband died of Yellow Fever, and Alexander Hamilton suffered through typhoid. George Washington was inaugurated in 1789 in a New York City recently ravaged by a pandemic. And yet, as well aware as they were, they did not make provisions to strip rights away in the event of disease.

There is an inexorable link between death and freedom. The philosopher Martin Heidegger put it this way, "If I take death into my life, acknowledge it, and face it squarely, I will free myself from the anxiety of death and the pettiness of life—and only then will I be free to become myself." In some ways, this is the foundational concept of Christianity and Christendom, or as we call it now, the West. Not only is death essential to the concept of freedom in Christianity, but it is only through death and resurrection that freedom is even possible.

At least since middle of the 20th century, Americans have lived at a distance from death. For a thousand previous generations, children saw grandparents grow old and die in the home. It was a natural process and part of everyday life. When I worked as a mover, I often noticed that most Brooklyn Brownstown buildings have a little nook carved into the bend of the stairway. Curious about it, I looked into it one day, and they are called "coffin corners." It was a way to get a coffin up the stairs when somebody died. Today, our kids visit their elderly relatives in old folks homes until eventually they die and there is a funeral. We protect kids in a way by doing this, but protect them from what exactly?

When I talked to Tucker Carlson about this, he had this to say, "I really think that the hysteria and the truly unreasonable behavior, the inability to make rational decisions you know all these very ugly things you're seeing on display right now, they are way deeper than politics. All of them grow out of the society's collective unwillingness to address the most basic question, which is what happens when you die…if we don't have any theory on it—that causes insanity and it causes people to, it causes people to believe that the highest good, like, really, the only job of our society, of government is to extend life or preserve life indefinitely. And that's not just unrealistic, it's insane and it allows for lots of other things like this."

A society that has no way to handle the concept of death will always struggle with the concepts of freedom and liberty. Freedom is at its core all about risk. It is not just that a free person can pursue what they desire, but that they can put everything on the line, even their own life, to achieve it. As Donald Rumsfeld once put it, "Free people are free to make mistakes, and commit crimes and do bad things, they are also free to live their lives, and do wonderful things… We have to pick and choose, and to the extent you pick and choose and you're wrong, the penalty can be enormous."

This balance between freedom and death, this struggle that weaves its way through the history of mankind and his ideas, was apparent at the earliest moments of the American experiment. In 1620, when the Pilgrims landed, they knew that death was a likely outcome, and indeed, many died. This would be true for wave after wave of arrivals, and true of the settling of the West. That preference for freedom over safety lingered. This is why our gun rights baffle even the nations that are most similar to us in the world. Americans know that we could adopt the restrictive measures of other nations and drastically reduce gun deaths as they have. We don't do it because at least thus far, the freedom to bear arms has outweighed the risk of gun deaths for us.

Ultimately, the lockdowns of 2020 and the responses to them from the American people announced a new moment of

21st-century culture war. Just a year earlier, in 2019, the *New York Times* would put out its 1619 project to coincide with the first slave ships reaching America. The project was an attempt to reconstruct American history in such a way that the "founding" was not 1776 when Americans fought for and won their freedom from England, but 1619, when slavery began here. And this is, of course, part of a larger project to move America away from valuing individual liberty and toward valuing collective action aimed at ensuring the well-being of all.

What was shocking about the response from Americans to the lockdowns was how quickly they acquiesced to them and how little questioning of them our institutions allowed. This is owing in no small part to a new American Left that, over the past few decades, has abandoned the concept of classical liberalism. "I abhor your views but will die to protect your right to express them," has been replaced among progressives with the idea that speech is violence. That shift may seem remote from American's response to a deadly virus and the shut downs it led to, but it really isn't. More than anything else this devaluation of individual liberty explains why so many in our society, terrified of death, were willing not only to forgo their own rights, but far more importantly, to scold those who chose to exercise theirs.

What is required to stem this tide is a new conservative movement, one suited to battle with the new progressives. We need new and more aggressive approaches to almost every aspect of our politics, but a firm focus must be placed on education and religious life. And in this respect, in one term, Donald Trump provided his most profound legacy to help. The appointments of Neal Gorsuch, Brett Kavanaugh, and Amy Coney Barrett to the Supreme Court created a bulwark for the new Right, and an avenue to make important gains.

The ability for parents to use school choice to find education options not beholden to the new progressivism will be essential, but even in government school settings, the fight for school prayer and religious education must be rejoined. We must actively fight for a reading and understanding of our history that does not undermine the basic tenets of individual liberty. These are fights that have felt distant and esoteric in the past. The lockdown has taught us that they are not. That so many Americans have come to feel shame about what America has always been, a reckless experiment in freedom, has had devastating real-world consequences that almost nobody could have predicted back when the virus first made its way here from China.

The defense of American liberty by those not enthralled by the all-consuming fear of death will be the work of at least a generation, and signs don't look fantastic that it will be successful. On the other hand, it is quite possible that things look gloomier than they really are for lovers of freedom precisely because those who create our cultural content are disproportionately of an antiliberty mindset. This is exactly why if a new conservatism is to protect and defend the traditional values of America, it must do so not by catering to the whims of the elite, but by tapping into the power of unheard millions who support liberty without a corporate megaphone, but nonetheless support it.

Americans must choose freedom. We must understand that in this world of vast technology, from here going forward, there will always be advocates of isolation and atomization ready to benefit enormously from a compliant and pliant people. Today, it is a restaurant owner who loses her liquor license for opening her own business, or a rideshare company blacklisting riders who don't wear masks; tomorrow it will be social credit systems as we see in China: financial opportunities, the ability to speak freely, and travel meted out by governments and corporations that will punish those deemed to be too individualistic, not dedicated enough to their idea of the common good. And it will not be limited to infectious diseases.

After all, what is a public health crisis? It is whatever those in power say it is. Climate change is a public health crisis, racism is a public health crisis, defining gender with biology is a public health crisis. We have now set a dangerous precedent in this country that for nearly a year (at least), our basic liberties can be taken from us to combat a public health crisis. This includes not only our individual rights of assembly, worship, property, and movement, but also our most basic political right to be governed by elected officials under a system of checks and balances. Not by autocratic dictators with emergency powers. Even the fundamentals of federalism are under attack by those who demand that our responses to a public health crisis must be nationalized, that states must not be allowed to choose their responses.

What is at stake in all of this is nothing short of the American experiment itself. And yes, it is a dangerous experiment; it always has been. Its primary goal is not the preservation of life but for individuals to be able to decide for themselves how to live their lives, even at times when it endangers themselves and others. Freedom is perilous and yet is also the birthright of every American. Had the founders valued the protection of life at all costs over freedom, there would never have been a United States of America. They did not merely pledge their honor and fortunes to freedom and liberty, but also their lives.

As the heirs to the American Revolution, the Declaration of Independence, and the Constitution, we are not merely blessed by also burdened. Freedom is a burden; it is a challenge precisely because we must make choices without any promise that we are choosing wisely. Freedom cannot exist in a society where science and expertise may compel myriad restrictive behaviors on an unwilling population, even in an effort to save lives. Thus, Americans have come to a time of choosing, because this will not be the last public health crisis. Taken all in all, the evidence is clear that we must never choose to lock down this way again. No. We must choose liberty, we must remain the flickering flame of freedom that promises to light the world. We are Americans, but if we continue to allow the erosion of rights at time of supposed emergency, we will not be Americans for long. We will become something else, and should that happen, our loss of freedom will be the worst casualty of the Chinese virus. Let us pledge that that will never happen.

About the Author

D avid Marcus is the New York correspondent for *The Federalist* and a columnist for the *New York Post*. Born and raised in Philadelphia, he now resides in Brooklyn.

ENDNOTES

1 Global Health Security Index, "2019 GHS Country Index Profile for United States," accessed May 10, 2021, https://www.ghsindex.org/country/united-states/.

2 Eileen Drage O'Reilly, "China Hunts Cause of Mysterious Pneumonia Outbreak in Wuhan," Axios, January 6, 2020, https://www.axios.com/china-pneumonia-oubtreak-wuhan-e2ef8914-6bd7-46db-814d-1609d590ee07.html.

3 Health Emergency Office, "Notification of Wuhan Municipal Health Commission on Unexplained Viral Pneumonia," National Health Commission of the People's Republic of China, January 11, 2020, http://www.nhc.gov.cn/xcs/yqtb/202001/1beb46f061704372b7ca 41ef3e682229.shtml.

4 Health Emergency Office, "Notification of Wuhan Municipal Health Commission on Pneumonia Caused by New Coronavirus Infection," National Health Commission of the People's Republic of China, January 13, 2020, http://www.nhc.gov.cn/xcs/yqtb/202001/8254506a10fe490eae755 66b02a51793.shtml.

5 World Health Organization (@WHO), "Preliminary investigations conducted by the Chinese authorities have found no clear evidence of human-to-human transmission of the novel #coronavirus (2019-nCoV) identified in #Wuhan, #China," Twitter, January 14, 2020, 5:18 a.m., https://twitter.com/WHO/status/1217043229427761152.

6 CDC, "Transcript of 2019 Novel Coronavirus Response Telebriefing," Centers for Disease Control and Prevention, January 17, 2020, https://www.cdc.gov/media/releases/2020/t0117-coronavirus-screening.html.

271

[7] CDC, "Interim Guidelines for Collecting and Handling of Clinical Specimens for COVID-19 Testing," accessed May 9, 2021, https://www.cdc.gov/coronavirus/2019-ncov/lab/guidelines-clinical-specimens.html.

[8] CDC, "Interim Laboratory Biosafety Guidelines for Handling and Processing Specimens Associated with Coronavirus Disease 2019 (COVID-19)," accessed May 9, 2021, https://www.cdc.gov/coronavirus/2019-ncov/lab/lab-biosafety-guidelines.html.

[9] CDC, "Interim Guidance for Implementing Home Care of People Not Requiring Hospitalization for Coronavirus Disease 2019 (COVID-19)," updated October 16, 2020, accessed May 9, 2021, https://www.cdc.gov/coronavirus/2019-ncov/hcp/guidance-home-care.html.

[10] Lily Kuo, "China Confirms Human-to-Human Transmission of Coronavirus," *The Guardian*, January 20, 2020, https://www.theguardian.com/world/2020/jan/20/coronavirus-spreads-to-beijing-as-china-confirms-new-cases.

[11] CDC, "Transcript of Update on 2019 Novel Coronavirus (2019-nCoV)," January 21, 2020, accessed May 9, 2021, https://www.cdc.gov/media/releases/2020/t0121-Telebriefing-Coronavirus.html.

[12] CDC, "If You Are Sick or Caring for Someone," updated November 20, 2020, accessed May 9, 2021, https://www.cdc.gov/coronavirus/2019-ncov/if-you-are-sick/index.html.

[13] Fox Business, "Deadly Contagion in China Spreads to the US," January 22, 2020, video clip, 05:20, https://video.foxbusiness.com/v/6125383849001#sp=show-clips.

[14] Anna Fifield and Lena H. Sun, "Travel Ban Goes into Effect in Chinese City of Wuhan as Authorities Try to Stop Coronavirus Spread," *The Washington Post*, January 22, 2020, https://www.washingtonpost.com/world/asia_pacific/nine-dead-as-chinese-coronavirus-spreads-despite-efforts-to-contain-it/2020/01/22/1eaade72-3c6d-11ea-afe2-090eb37b60b1_story.html.

15 CDC, "Transcript of 2019 Novel Coronavirus Response," updated January 24, 2020, accessed May 9, 2021, https://www.cdc.gov/media/releases/2020/t0124-Telebriefing-Coronavirus.html.

16 U.S. Department of Health and Human Services, "HHS Leadership," accessed May 9, 2021, https://www.hhs.gov/about/leadership/index.html.

17 CDC, "Transcript of 2019 Novel Coronavirus (2019-nCoV) Update," January 27, 2020, accessed May 9, 2021, https://www.cdc.gov/media/releases/2020/t0127-coronavirus-update.html.

18 U.S. Food and Drug Administration, "FDA Announces Key Actions to Advance Development of Novel Coronavirus Medical Countermeasures," January 27, 2020, accessed May 9, 2021, https://www.fda.gov/news-events/press-announcements/fda-announces-key-actions-advance-development-novel-coronavirus-medical-countermeasures.

19 U.S. Department of Health and Human Services, "HHS Leadership," accessed May 9, 2021, https://www.hhs.gov/about/leadership/index.html.

20 CDC, "Updated Interim Guidance for Airlines and Airline Crew: Coronavirus Disease 2019 (COVID-19)," updated March 4, 2020, accessed May 9, 2021, https://www.cdc.gov/quarantine/air/managing-sick-travelers/ncov-airlines.html.

21 CDC, "Transcript of 2019 Novel Coronavirus (2019-nCoV) Response," January 29, 2020, accessed May 9, 2021, https://www.cdc.gov/media/releases/2020/t0129-cdc-telebriefing-2019-novel-coronavirus.html.

22 CDC, "Interim Infection Prevention and Control Recommendations for Healthcare Personnel During the Coronavirus Disease 2019 (COVID-19) Pandemic," updated February 23, 2021, accessed May 9, 2021, https://www.cdc.gov/coronavirus/2019-ncov/hcp/infection-control-recommendations.html.

[23] Jeremy Hobson and Francesca Paris, "Couple Remains under Quarantine in Texas after Honeymoon on the Diamond Princess," WBUR, February 20, 2020, https://www.wbur.org/hereandnow/2020/02/20/coronavirus-covid-19-quarantine-diamond-princess.

[24] CDC, "Transcript of CDC Telebriefing for the Update on 2019 Novel Coronavirus (2019-nCoV)," January 30, 2020, accessed May 9, 2021, https://www.cdc.gov/media/releases/2020/t0130-novel-coronavirus-update-telebriefing.html.

[25] CDC, "CDC Confirms Seventh Case of 2019 Novel Coronavirus," January 31, 2020, accessed May 9, 2021, https://www.cdc.gov/media/releases/2020/s0131-seventh-case-coronavirus.html.

[26] Talia Kaplan, "HHS Secretary Azar on Coronavirus: 'We Will Take All...Measures Necessary to Protect the American Public," Fox News, January 30, 2020, 'https://www.foxnews.com/media/hhs-secretary-azar-leading-coronavirus-task-force-to-address-us-response-to-outbreak.

[27] U.S. Department of Health and Human Services, "Secretary Azar Declares Public Health Emergency for United States for 2019 Novel Coronavirus," January 31, 2020, accessed May 9, 2021, https://www.hhs.gov/about/news/2020/01/31/secretary-azar-declares-public-health-emergency-us-2019-novel-coronavirus.html.

[28] U.S. Department of Health and Human Services, "HHS Leadership," accessed May 9, 2021, https://www.hhs.gov/about/leadership/index.html.

[29] Patrick Chovanec (@prchovanec), "I mean, if we hand out too many ventilators, people might prefer it to breathing on their own," Twitter, March 26, 2020, 9:09 p.m., https://twitter.com/prchovanec/status/1243359511743574022.

[30] Katie Way, "Cuomo's Prison Workers Say They're Not Actually Making Hand Sanitizer," *Vice*, March 25, 2020, https://www.vice.com/en_us/article/5dma4k/cuomos-prison-workers-say-theyre-not-actually-making-hand-sanitizer.

[31] Julia Marsh, "De Blasio Is 'Making a Lot of Mistakes' with Coronavirus Response: Sources," *The New York Post*, March 15,

2020, https://nypost.com/2020/03/15/de-blasio-is-making-a-lot-of-mistakes-with-coronavirus-response-sources/.

32 David Marcus, "We Cannot Destroy the Country for the Sake of New York City," *The Federalist*, April 3, 2020, https://thefederalist.com/2020/04/03/we-cannot-destroy-the-country-for-the-sake-of-new-york-city/.

33 David Weigel, "The Trailer: The Resistance to Stay-at-Home Orders Rises from the Right," *The Washington Post*, April 16, 2020, https://www.washingtonpost.com/politics/paloma/the-trailer/2020/04/16/the-trailer-the-resistance-to-stay-at-home-orders-rises-from-the-right/5e970f46602ff10d49ae5b2a/.

34 Media Matters Staff, "Tucker Carlsen Praises the Michigan Protest against Coronavirus Mitigation Efforts," Media Matters for America, April 15, 2020, https://www.mediamatters.org/tucker-carlson/tucker-carlson-praises-michigan-protest-against-coronavirus-mitigation-efforts.

35 Bobby Lewis (@revrrlewis), "Brian Kilmeade predicts that "as more and more states go online and get their rights back," it will spawn a larger movement against "ridiculous" stay-at-home orders. Andrew Napolitano also accuses the New Jersey governor of felony misconduct, "an impeachable offense," Twitter, April 16, 2020, 6;19 a.m., https://twitter.com/revrrlewis/status/1250745738503557120?ref_src=twsrc%5Etfw%7Ctwcamp%5Etweetembed%7Ctwterm%5E1250745738503557120&ref_url=https%3A%2F%2Fwww.mediamatters.org%2Ffox-news%2Ffox-news-promoting-protests-against-social-distancing-measures-god-bless-them.

36 Lis Power (@LisPower1), "Fox anchor Harris Faulkner on the Michigan protests that ignored social distancing guidelines and put *others* in danger. Faulkner: 'This country was kind of founded on people who were willing to risk themselves for freedom, is that what this is, or something else?'" Twitter, April 16, 2020, 12:23 p.m., https://mobile.twitter.com/LisPower1/status/1250837228420554753

37 Thomas Levinson, "Social Distancing in the Sun: The *Post*'s Week in Photos," *New York Post*, May 8, 2020,

https://nypost.com/2020/05/08/social-distancing-in-the-sun-the-posts-week-in-photos/.

[38] Jon Levine, "Some Georgia Restaurant Owners Refuse to Reopen as Coronavirus Lockdown Ends," *New York Post*, May 2, 2020, https://nypost.com/2020/05/02/georgia-restaurant-owners-refuse-to-reopen-as-lockdown-ends/.

[39] Amanda Mull, "Georgia's Experiment in Human Sacrifice," *The Atlantic*, April 29, 2020, https://www.theatlantic.com/health/archive/2020/04/why-georgia-reopening-coronavirus-pandemic/610882/.